Advance praise for *Out of Exile*...

At the end of 2013, I was hurt and wounded as I had never been in over 20 years of pastoral ministry. I was disillusioned, out of work, and a complete mess. But then, somehow, I stumbled on your "Out of Exile" writings. And wow... did God use it to restore my soul. I worked through the first 24 days of your writing in about two days, then reviewed and reviewed and reviewed various sections for the next two or three months. God used your writings to significantly restore my soul, my faith in the church, and my internal perspective on God. Even my wife and our two sons regularly said, "What in the world are you reading? You are a different man than you were before."

Thank you for allowing God's inspiration to flow through you. Your thoughts, your encouragements, your challenges were timely and necessary to rebuild in me what had been lost. I'd had an amazingly charmed ministry experience up to this point -- I was loved, appreciated, sought after, and though I had certainly faced challenges from time to time in our various churches/ministry experiences, was woefully unprepared for the evil, vile hatred expressed toward us in this overwhelmingly difficult season of ministry. I wanted to quit, not just on the church, but on God as well.

God used you to keep me in ministry. I owe you a huge debt, and I don't even know you. Thank you!

Ken DePeal
Olathe, Kansas
2014

D1606554

OUT of EXILE

A Forty Day Journey
From Setback to Comeback

PASTORS EDITION

F. REMY DIEDERICH

Out of Exile: A Forty Day Journey from Setback to Comeback
By F. Remy Diederich

For more great content from F. Remy Diederich, visit his website at:
www.readingremy.com

Cover Design by: Jason M. Brooks www.jasonmbrooks.com/book-publishing
Author photo courtesy of: Angie Green www.angiegreen.com

A Special thank you to Emelia Roso for editing the content of this manuscript.

Be Sure To Check Out These Other Titles From F. Remy Diederich

Healing the Hurts of Your Past:
A Guide to Overcoming the Pain of Shame

ISBN: 978-0-615-535463
www.readingremy.com/healing

Stuck:
How to Overcome Your Anger and Reclaim Your Life

ISBN: 978-0-615-740072
www.readingremy.com/stuck

TABLE OF CONTENTS

This book is dedicated to the countless pastors living in exile who wonder if they will ever find their way back to a fruitful ministry.

This is what the LORD says: "When seventy years are completed for Babylon, I will come to you and fulfill my gracious promise to bring you back to this place. For I know the plans I have for you," declares the LORD, "plans to prosper you and not to harm you, plans to give you hope and a future. Then you will call upon me and come and pray to me, and I will listen to you. You will seek me and find me when you seek me with all your heart. I will be found by you," declares the LORD, "and will bring you back from captivity. I will gather you from all the nations and places where I have banished you," declares the LORD, "and will bring you back to the place from which I carried you into exile."

Jeremiah 29:10-14

INTRODUCTION

Exile is when life throws you a curve, and you end up in a place you never thought possible. You feel stuck and fear you will never get back on track: a washout for God.

In the fall of 2013, I spoke at a pastors retreat on the theme of exile. My teaching hit a nerve. Pastors could relate. Many had experienced exile or were currently in one. It was comforting for them to see they were not alone. What they experienced was not unique. God had not abandoned them. In fact, all of God's people are people of exile in one form or another: at one time or another. Hearing this normalized their experience and showed them a way to return from exile.

After the retreat, I released the material with additional thoughts in forty posts on my blog (readingremy.com) over a four-month period, calling it: Out of Exile: *a forty-day journey for hurting pastors.* Again, it hit a nerve. Many readers asked me to spin the posts into a book and so that is what you are holding now.

What exactly is exile? Exile is when life throws you a curve, and you end up in a place you never thought possible. You feel stuck and fear you will never get back on track: a washout for God.

When pastors respond to God's call, most of us think we will save the world, but too often we end up on the backside of a desert. That's not the worst thing. In many ways, it's a rite of passage: a preparation for ministry to come. But too many pastors get stuck in exile. We lose our bearings and have no idea how to reclaim our lives or ministry.

In the coming pages, I will look at the losses all pastors' face in ministry, how the losses create a feeling of "exile," and then how to return from that exile. This book is set up as a 40-day devotional: short essays followed by questions to help you move through your time of loss to a place of restoration.[1]

I want to get you thinking and talking about your losses. The best part of the pastors' retreat was the conversations it sparked and the permission it gave pastors to talk about their exile. So don't keep this to yourself. Process what you learn with your husband or wife, children, friends and fellow pastors. Many pastors and their spouses thanked me for giving them new terms for their experience of exile: a common language to talk about their feelings. I think you will find similar benefits as you work your way through this forty-day journey.

---

[1] Even though this is written to pastors, it applies to all people and will help everyone learn how to process their losses in life.

Don't rush through this book. Let it peel back the layers of hurt that have accumulated for years. Then invite God's Spirit to bring healing and wisdom.

F. Remy Diederich, June 2014

DAY 1

HOW DID I GET HERE?

As much as I believed in the church, nothing felt right. I wondered if I could ever join a church again or be in ministry. I'll never forget the sense of "otherness" I felt during that time.

As I said in the introduction, exile is how you feel when life throws you a curve and you end up in a place you never imagined you'd be. You look around and ask yourself: *How on earth did I get here?*

I've gone through my share of exiles. Thankfully, I've come out the other side. But beyond returning, God actually used my exiles to shape me and prepare me for the ministry I'm enjoying now. Without my times of exile I would probably have a small church of closed-minded, judgmental people, or be out of the ministry altogether. But exile changed me. It broadened me, enabling me to relate to many more people than in my pre-exile days.

My Five Exiles

To start our journey, I want to give you some context for how I came to learn what I'll be sharing with you. I won't tell my whole story, but I briefly want to outline five "exiles"

I've gone through, using five descriptive words. I bet you can relate to at least one of them.

Scandal: I came to faith in a large upbeat charismatic church in the 70's. Their success got the best of them. It fell apart after the pastor was exposed in an affair. A church of over 2000 people was scattered to the four winds. It doesn't even exist today. The church had no idea how to handle the pastor's failure. Factions polarized over whether to restore the pastor or throw him out. It was pure chaos. Up until that time, my faith was black and white. I had it all mapped out. I was in a perfect church, but the scandal turned my world upside down. I didn't know what to think. The things that were once black and white turned to grey.

Control: Looking for some sanity, I attended a small church that got started out of the large church. I was convinced a small church was the answer to the chaos that happened there. At the small church, I knew the pastor personally. We were friends, neighbors, and I trusted him. He mentored me to learn a trade to help support me in ministry. And he invited me to work part-time for the church, giving me my first chance at "professional" ministry. It was great. I knew everyone in the church. It was a close-knit family. Faith made sense again.

But over time my friend and pastor became increasingly paranoid and controlling. I anguished over what to do. I tried to talk to him, but he didn't see what I was saying. Finally, after receiving two visions of warning, he told the congregation that if they left the church something bad would happen to them.

This situation was too much. I confronted him about his visions, paranoia, and the negative approach he had taken. His response was that I could agree with him or leave. I left the church, hurt and disillusioned.

Isolation: When my wife and I left the church, we were cut off from our closest friends. We didn't want to cause them problems with the pastor or incite them to take up our offense, so we kept our distance from them. The loss of our community was intense. One day I played some worship music we used to sing in church. I was overcome with a deep sense of grief. I had lost something I couldn't get back.

Then something strange happened inside of us: church suddenly became shallow and cliché. As much as I believed in church, nothing about it felt right. Every few weeks we would try another church to see if we had "gotten over it." But it was always the same. It was the oddest feeling: like strangers in a strange land where everyone spoke a different language. I'll never forget the sense of "otherness" I felt during that time. I wondered if I could ever join a church again or be in ministry. I longed for fellowship with believers but felt totally alone.

Dysfunction: Not knowing what to do with our new condition, my wife and I gave up on church and moved into a community with two other families. We were confident we could love each other, love Jesus, and live out our faith with fewer people involved. How could anything go wrong with such like-minded people in such an idyllic place (a farm in Wisconsin)? You would be amazed how much can go wrong! We disbanded after seven years of agonizing through the intensity of our dysfunctional relationships.

Repression: Toward the end of our farm experience I realized that giving up on church was not the answer. We left the farm and reentered church life where I served as an associate pastor in a somewhat traditional and conservative church. At the time I accepted the position, I didn't realize I was wired to be a lead pastor. The church was fine, but serving as an associate when I had a heart to lead proved to be very frustrating, and yet another exile. I was confused about what God wanted me to do. I felt called to ministry but serving as an associate pastor in a conservative church was boring. I felt boxed in. My poor wife had to listen to me lament about my dissatisfaction week after week.

There are many other smaller exiles that I've experienced, but I wanted to mention enough to give you an idea of what I'm talking about with exile. Now it's time for you to reflect on your exiles.

What about you?

- *Can you think of other types of exile, other than the ones I mentioned?*

- *What are some words that capture your exile experiences?*

- *How many exiles have you experienced? What were they?*

DAY 2

THE FIVE "D'S" OF EXILE

I was afraid the few good experiences I had were gone forever, and I would never enter a true move of God again.

In addition to the five exiles I listed in Day One, here are five words that describe how I felt in exile:

Displaced – Exile feels like being ripped from the safety of your home: uprooted and cast out. This was especially true when I first left the large church. It was the only church I had known up to that point. I lost my bearings. I was disoriented. Coming to faith helped me "find myself," but losing the church that helped me find faith made me question everything again.

Disconnected – Once displaced, I was alone. No peers. No family. No tribe. No one who spoke my "language," that is, identified with my experience. I thought my experience was unique. It reminds me of Tim Allen's story (the comedian). In describing his childhood, Tim said that when his father died no one seemed to understand his pain. It was like he was in a boat adrift, all alone.

Disillusioned – Church left me confused for many years. Biblically, I was a believer and understood I was a part of God's Church: his family. But experientially, I was an orphan and that didn't make any sense to me. Why would God allow this to happen? I had been told my church was "right." It was a New Testament church, just like in the Bible. We had an inside track. We saw things other believers didn't see. Not only did that church fail, but every other expression of church I tried, whether small church or community, failed as well. I was desperate to find a model that worked, but feared there were no answers out there.

Depressed – The lie of loss is: *life will never be good again*. That's how I felt about church and ministry. I was afraid the few good experiences I did have, were gone forever, and I would never enter a true move of God again. It put a cloud over my entire life. I didn't know who I was without the church.

Full of Doubt – A big part of my experience at the traditional church, where I came back into ministry, was the lack of people who saw what I saw. My ideas were continually shot down and told they would never work. (It wasn't until much later when we started Cedarbrook Church that we were able to implement my ideas and found great success. I felt exonerated.) This happens to young innovators all the time. Their ideas are seen as foolish or threatening, and it causes them to question their thinking. That's what happened to me. The experience filled me with doubt. I wondered if people were right. Maybe I didn't know what I was talking about. It made me want to quit many times.

Thankfully, God sent people my way to encourage me (more on that later) so I didn't give up.

What about you?

- *Can you relate to these words? How so?*

- *What are some other words that define your exile experience? (They don't have to start with "D!")*

FIVE REASONS FOR ENDING UP IN EXILE

It helps to know what landed you in exile. It's not always your fault.

People often think that sin is the only cause for ending up in exile. But that is just one reason. I can think of five reasons why people might end up in exile:

Unbelief: When God's people failed to enter the Promised Land they doubted God's ability to help them. As a result, God let them remain in the Wilderness, their exile, for forty years until that generation died out. They chose to stay in a barren desert rather than take the risk God called them to take.

Sometimes doubt strands us in a place we never wanted to be. Maybe that's happened to you: God asked you to do something but you refused out of fear and now you are in a no-man's-land: an exile you created by not moving forward when God asked it of you.

When I lived on our farm, I felt God tell me that it was time to move. But then I doubted. I thought there might be a way to make things work, after all, we had invested so much emotionally and financially. How could I just walk away? Six months later I was desperate in prayer, asking God what he wanted me to do. More clearly than ever I sensed God say: *I already told you what to do.* I immediately remembered my previous sense that God wanted us to move. Doubt had frozen me in place, and almost robbed me of what God was calling us to do. My wife and I immediately set plans in motion to move.

Sin and Rebellion. Once God's people made it into the Promised Land, they again lost the right to live there: this time for worshipping false gods. People turned to false gods when the competing religion promised something they didn't believe God could deliver: a good harvest, fertility, financial blessing, revenge, etc. God spoke through Ezekiel saying:

> ...the children rebelled against me: They did not follow my decrees, they were not careful to keep my laws... and they desecrated my Sabbaths. So I said I would pour out my wrath on them and spend my anger against them in the desert. But I withheld my hand, and for the sake of my name ... I swore to them in the desert that I would disperse them among the nations and scatter them through the countries, because they had not obeyed my laws but had rejected my decrees and desecrated my Sabbaths, and their eyes [lusted] after their fathers' idols. Ezekiel 20:21-24

Maybe you've done the same thing; only it's not false religion you've turned to for relief. Maybe you've sought out your own pleasure instead of pleasing God. You thought you were justified in going your own way because you had it so bad. Your worship shifted from God to cheap substitutes, vices of pleasure that became the new center for your life and devotion.

Bad Choices. Bad choices aren't about unbelief or rebellion. You just made some decisions that set you back and put you in a season of exile. Maybe you made bad financial choices that got you in trouble. Maybe you said things that got you in hot water and put your job or marriage in jeopardy. Or maybe you allowed yourself to get too busy, and the stress of it caused you to burn out or lose connection to your family.

Bad Luck. Some people end up in exile through no fault of their own. Sometimes bad things just happen for no reason. Tragedy, of all kind, falls into this category.

God's call. Sometimes God calls us to a hard place. It's not for any of the reasons above. It's just that God's will can't be accomplished in any other way than through suffering. God didn't spare Jesus from this. Jesus' suffering and crucifixion was the ultimate exile. For example, God may have called you to help a church go through a hard season. Someone has to do it. It's uphill all the way. God's not punishing you. He's using you to bring new life to this congregation.

I mention these five reasons for exile because it helps to know what landed you in exile so you will know what steps are necessary to find your way out.

What about you?

- *How did you end up in exile?*

- *Are there multiple reasons?*

- *How does knowing the cause help you discern the way out?*

DAY 4

LAID BARE

Exile is a metaphor for what God wants to do in his people. He uses exile to expose our true heart. He lays us bare.

I'm amazed at how many ex-pastors are still wandering in the wilderness, wondering what happened to them and having no idea how to get their lives back. Some of them have wandered for decades. Maybe you are one of them.

I have heard that only 5-10% of pastors *finish* their career in ministry. We all begin with visions of glory, but somewhere along the way most of us drop out, burn out, or get kicked out. What a sad statement. What's wrong with this picture? I hope this book will, in some small way, help at least a few pastors finish strong.

If you are in exile today, I want to help you find your way out. But to find the way out requires letting exile do its full work in you. Let me explain what I mean.

When God sent his people to Babylon in exile, he spoke to the prophet Ezekiel:

> *...son of man, pack your bags to prepare yourself for exile and **go into exile** (*galah*) ... Ezekiel 12:3*

The Hebrew word for "go into exile" is "galah." But "galah" also means to "expose, lay bare, uncover, reveal, be stripped." Here's another verse using "galah," but the word is translated "laid bare:"

> *I will tear down the wall you have covered with whitewash and will level it to the ground so that its foundation will be **laid bare** (galah).* Ezekiel 13:14

This means that exile isn't just a *physical* experience. Exile is also a metaphor for what God wants to do *inside* of you. He uses exile to expose your true heart. He "lays you bare," very much like this verse relates: he tears down everything false in you to expose your foundation. God allows hard times to reveal who you really are. He's not out to shame you. He wants to purify you by bringing your impurities to the surface and removing them.

Exile reveals your dark side (It can also reveal your good side). It has the unique ability to reveal things hidden deep within you that can't be found in good times. In order to move on from exile, it requires that you embrace the exile and let God do his full work in you. The more you resist it, the longer you stay in exile.

Think of it as spiritual surgery. The best thing you can do is lie still and let the surgeon do her work. Only then can the surgery be complete and you are allowed to move to the recovery room.

What about you?

- *What has exile revealed in your heart?*

- *How well have you done at "lying still" for God to do his work?*

- *What are some steps you might take after seeing what's in your heart?*

EXILE IS EVERYWHERE

It seems exile is a rite of passage for biblical greatness yet we dread it like The Plague.

You will be glad to know you are not the only one who has experienced exile. The Bible is full of exile stories.

Adam and Eve were exiled from the Garden of Eden. We've been trying to get back to the garden ever since. You could say that the entire human race is in exile for that reason.

The Flood was a time of exile for *Noah* as was the new life after the flood. He was cut off from everything he knew and had to struggle through being displaced.

Abraham was in exile in Canaan. Day Six will explore this more. *Hagar* was exiled from the presence of Abraham and Sarah. *Jacob* lived in exile under Laban's rule waiting to receive Rebecca as his wife. *Joseph* was in exile in the well and prison, while *Moses* was in exile many times: in the basket at birth, in the palace growing up, in the wilderness after killing a man, in the Sinai Wilderness, and in his lonely place of leadership.

David was in exile as he ran from *King Saul.* *Jonah* was in exile in the belly of the whale and in Ninevah. *God's* people were in exile in Egypt, Assyria, and Babylon. *Mary* was in exile as she faced the isolation of being pregnant out of wedlock and carrying a Child that no one understood.

Jesus was in exile when Satan tempted him, when no one understood him, as he prayed in Gethsemane, as he stood before his accusers, and as he hung on the cross. *Paul* was in exile from the Jews (once his greatest supporters) as well as when he endured his "thorn in the flesh." And *John* wrote his revelation in exile on the island of Patmos.

It's a wonder why we are so ignorant of exile, and God's purpose for it, when exile is so prevalent in the Bible. How can we be so blind? It seems exile is a rite of passage for biblical greatness, yet we dread it like The Plague.

If we fully understood how God uses exile to benefit us we would stand in line all night to get in this special "club," or pay a Harvard tuition to gain the wisdom it contains. But the good news is: we don't have to stand in line, or pay tuition for this education, do we? We all get a free scholarship; it's called "life." We just need to glean the wisdom from it that God has for us.

Why do we think exile is just for ancient times? If God used it then to prove his people, why wouldn't he use it now? He absolutely does. We can fight against it, or we can embrace it as the gift it is.

What about you?

- *Can you think of other exiles in the Bible?*

- *What has kept you from seeing the value of exile in your life?*

I DIDN'T SEE THIS COMING

When there's a famine in the land, you doubt your call or you doubt God's goodness, or both.

Today I want to look at one exile story in particular: Abram's. Anyone who is called of God can relate to his story:

> *The LORD had said to Abram, 'Leave your country, your people and your father's household and go to the land I will show you. I will make you into a great nation and I will bless you; I will make your name great, and you will be a blessing. I will bless those who bless you, and whoever curses you I will curse; and all peoples on earth will be blessed through you.' So Abram left, as the LORD had told him; and Lot went with him. Abram was seventy-five years old when he set out from Haran. He took his wife Sarai, his nephew Lot, all the possessions they had accumulated and the people they had acquired in Haran, and they set out for the land of Canaan, and they arrived there.* Genesis 12:1-5

As you read this story and reflect on your own ministry calling, what stands out to you? When I read Abram's story and compared it to God's calling on my life, I didn't think much about the cost of leaving what was familiar to me. I didn't think much about "being 75," that is, my limitations. I didn't think much about the "Lot's" in my life (unhealthy people) who would go with me. I focused on verse two. *"I will make you into a great nation and I will bless you; I will make your name great, and you will be a blessing."*

I bet that's what Abram heard too. How about you? I'm sure Abram was convinced Canaan would be amazing. Sarah probably wasn't so sure, but Abram was confident she'd come around once she saw what a great place it was.

In Canaan, Abram was going to establish God's kingdom. In Canaan, he was going to be the MAN, God's man. He was going to call the shots and make things happen in a way he never could as long as he was under his dad's oversight back in Haran. Canaan was definitely the land of promise! Abram couldn't get there fast enough.

Did you respond to God's call that way, that is, all you saw was the glory – the possibilities? But what did Abram find in Canaan?

> At that time the Canaanites were in the land. Genesis 12:6

Wait a minute. Canaanites? God never said anything about Canaanites. God never told me I'd have elders that disagreed with me, or worse, undermine me. God never told me I'd have members complain when new people came to the church, upsetting the balance of power. I thought God would send me to people that loved Jesus!

But that's not all Abram had to deal with. There's more. Or, I should say, less:

> *Now there was a famine in the land...* Genesis 12:10

A famine? If God called me, how could there be a famine? I thought God would take care of my needs. I shouldn't have to take a second job. I thought this would include a good health insurance plan. I thought I'd be able to afford a vacation.

And then came the doubts: *"Maybe I didn't hear God. Maybe that was just youthful ambition. Maybe that was zeal without knowledge...or bad onions for supper last night. I'm not so sure of what I'm doing."*

When there's a famine in the land, you doubt your call, or you doubt God's goodness, or both. There are many losses associated with the call of God. That's not bad. But it's important to name the losses, assess them, and grieve them; otherwise you will bury the pain of loss, and it will rot and smell and undermine your life and ministry. The process of managing your losses is what this journey is all about.

Too many pastors suffer loss but never deal with it. They put their head down, keep working, and "trust the Lord" that it will all work out. What they don't realize is that, by ignoring their losses, they are actually setting themselves up for exile later...and many never return.

What about you?

- *What were some of your expectations for ministry that haven't been met?*

- *What are some losses you've encountered that you never saw coming?*

- *How have these losses affected you...really?*

EMBRACING YOUR DARK SIDE

We are all Abram before God transforms us into Abraham.

Let's keep looking at Abram's early days. I'm speculating that Abram was excited at God's call to move to Canaan. He was full of hope with visions of changing the world for God. But when he got to Canaan he was met with two unexpected companions: Canaanites and famine. He didn't see them coming.

So maybe it shouldn't surprise us that as soon as Abram arrived in Canaan, he quickly felt compelled to leave.

> *Abram went down to Egypt to live there for a while because the famine was severe.* Genesis 12:10

I wonder if you've ever done that...left some place soon after you got there? The "famine" was too great. You didn't know what you had bargained for. You thought you heard from God but then everything was so foreign: so hard. You became disillusioned and looked for a way out. Sometimes it's easier to just leave and start over.

I have a young friend, Sam, who joined a church out of seminary. The church had an aging pastor headed for retirement, and they were looking to bring in some fresh blood to attract younger families. The pastor was eager to share his leadership, and the governing board promised to support new ideas, so Sam took the job with visions of a smooth transition.

Can you guess what happened? Everyone sang a different song once Sam was on staff. His ideas were too controversial to the board, and the pastor didn't want to give up control. In fact, he thought he had a few more years left in him. Sam was crushed and wondered if he missed God by taking this position. He's anguished over what to do and is currently considering leaving.

That's what Abram did. He left Canaan. But look what happened when he got to Egypt. He was afraid Pharaoh would kill him, and take his wife, so he told his wife:

> *Please say that you're my sister. Then everything will be all right for me, and because of you I will live.* Genesis 12:13

This is a nice way to say, *"Please prostitute yourself to save my butt."* Pharaoh was always looking to add another beautiful woman to his harem, and that's what he did when he saw Sarah. Abram did two things that he probably never thought he'd do: lie and sellout his wife. How could this happen? What could drive him to do these things? Exile.

Exile puts you to the test and brings out your dark side (and sometimes it's your dark side that puts you into exile.) That's one of the main reasons we hate it so much. Not only do we hate the "Canaanites" and the "famine," we hate seeing the ugly way we respond to the stress and temptation of exile. We like to think we are better than that; we are above that. This is where many people turn to denial to salve their pain. But the bold and the brave embrace their dark side and invite God to do his work in them.

Abram's story was given by God to help everyone called by God. We are all Abram before God transforms us into Abraham. Exile is what enabled God to transform Abram (father) to Abraham (father of many) and call him his friend. Imagine what God might do in you?

What about you?

- *Have you ever left a job, relationship, etc. that you felt called to, but couldn't handle it? What were the losses that caused you to leave?*

- *How have your exiles exposed your dark side? What specifically was revealed?*

- *How did you handle that? Did you face your dark side, run from it, or cover it up?*

DAY 8

EIGHT CATEGORIES OF EXILE

There is no quick fix to exile. It's like a seed in the ground. It needs to suffer many days in the dark before something is birthed, grows, and bears fruit.

Today is the last day of defining exile. In days to come I'll look at what we learn in exile and then ultimately, how to return from exile. Be patient. I know you want to find a way out, but there is no quick fix to exile. It's like a seed in the ground. It needs to suffer many days in the dark before something is birthed, grows, and bears fruit.

We typically think of exile as being when people leave their country. But as I said before, living in exile isn't just about being displaced. There are many aspects to exile. Earlier I spoke about five specific types of exile. Today I want to explore eight general categories of exile:

Emotional: There's a dark side to our emotions such as; depression, post-traumatic stress (PTSD), anxiety, panic attacks, bipolar disorder, and many others. One commenter to my blog series said he struggled for years with the exile of addiction until he was diagnosed as bi-polar, which changed his life. His life was a barren wilderness until he was put on medication that delivered him from his addiction.

Spiritual: Many people struggle seeking and finding God. For some, it's natural. For others, God is confusing and covered in clouds. Some have called their separation from God their "dark night of the soul." Bad church experiences or bad encounters with "spiritual" people can add to this confusion and disillusionment.

Relational: God created us for relationships. When our relationships break down or never happen to begin with, they can consume us. Divorce, estrangement from children/parents, death of a loved one, and bad marriages are just a few of the relational exiles we experience.

Financial: Nothing consumes us quicker than the loss of income. It immediately grabs our attention and insists on controlling every waking thought.

Career: Looking for work can feel like exile, especially if it goes on for an extended period of time. You begin to feel like an orphan without a home or identity, not to mention the financial stress. It's especially hard for ministers because they get into this "line of work" from what they thought was a call from God. If they can't find work, what does that say about their calling? If they accept a secular job are they letting God down? But if they finally find a job and it turns out to be a bad match (like for my friend Sam) is it right to leave and start over?

Physical: We take our health for granted until it leaves us. Wrestling with chronic pain, burnout, injuries, the inability to have children, or terminal diseases are just a few examples of problems that can lead to a sense of exile. I've always been healthy but over the last year I've had a few physical struggles (phantom fatigue and sports injuries). I'm surprised how much it has affected me emotionally. My inability to do what I want to do, at the level I want to do it, has proven to be a big loss for me.

Season of life: Transitions between seasons of life might seem minor, but they often surprise us and leave us in exile. Marriage, childbirth, the empty nest, the time between college and marriage and a career, retirement, and managing old age can all present exile experiences.

Success: This might not be obvious, but success can lead to a transition in life you aren't prepared for. I've experienced some ministry success that I didn't anticipate. When I achieved results that went beyond what I ever imagined, I was disoriented for a number of months and even depressed. I achieved what I wanted and didn't know what to do next. I lost my purpose for a season before getting refocused on the next phase of my life.

What about you?

- *How many categories impact you?* Rank them in order of impact on you.

- *What do you think the compounding impact is on your life?*

- *Can you think of other categories of exile?*

EXPERIENCING LOSS

Most of us are ill prepared for loss and I'm not sure why that is. Are we that optimistic or that naive?

I want to look at what sends you into exile in the first place.

Of course, outright sin is the fast track to exile. Many ministers have had moral failures that sidelined them for years. But what I want to do here is to focus on more of the subtle causes of exile.

What sends you into exile is loss. I've talked about loss a bit already. Loss happens when your experience falls short of your expectation. If you look back over the last few days, that's what happened to Abram. He expected glory. He experienced famine. That was a loss.

EXPECTATION

LOSS

EXPERIENCE

Most of us are ill prepared for loss and I'm not sure that is. Are we that optimistic, or that naive? We see loss all around us. But we rarely think it will happen to us. When it does, we are often devastated and disillusioned. It can knock us off course and into exile for years.

Loss produces a variety of uncomfortable emotions. The big three are:

- **Anger**- you are mad that your expectation wasn't met; mad at whomever you think is responsible.

- **Sadness**- you mourn the loss of what you expected to have forever.

- **Fear** – you are afraid that you will never achieve your expectation: that loss will be a way of life from now on.

These emotions are normal. In fact, they are good. If you didn't have an emotional response to loss, there would be something wrong with you. We have a word for people who do not show normal emotions: *sociopath*. So be glad you have emotions. God gave you emotions to move you to resolve your problems.

But, be careful; don't get stuck in your emotions; *move through* them to a better place. Don't stuff your emotion as a "quick-fix" to their discomfort. And don't vent them thinking that's how you get release. Explore your emotions to help you learn what's going on inside your head and heart.

Your emotions give you a clue to wrong - even toxic - thinking that might be present within you. When your emotions fire, ask God to use them to pinpoint trouble spots that require healing.

What about you?

- *What are some emotions you've experienced from loss?*

- *How do you handle your emotions? Do you try to suppress them or vent them?*

- *What have you learned about yourself and God from your emotions?*

DENYING YOUR LOSS

For some, sin leads them into exile.
For others, exile is what leads them to sin.

Anger, fear, and sadness operate like a *Band of Brothers*. It's almost impossible to have one without the other. That's why it's important you learn to identify them in your life and have a plan to deal with each one.

Unfortunately, a quick solution to these emotions is denial. Feel bad? No problem. Just immerse yourself in behavior that drowns out the noise from your loss.

We've all been there. Denial looks different to everybody. It can be socially acceptable behavior, like working too much, or over-indulging in hobbies, or exercise, or "social" drinking. But for too many, it goes way beyond socially acceptable. Exile brings such strong disillusionment people feel justified in throwing off any inhibitions they once had and dive headlong into alcohol and drug abuse, pornography, an affair, misuse of funds, or any behavior that helps them escape the pain of their loss.

Their misguided thinking says: *If life doesn't make sense, then why bother trying to keep the rules?* That's why we are often shocked to learn about the secret lifestyles of people who were once known for their integrity and moral influence. For some, sin leads them into exile. For others, exile is what leads them to sin.

The most common form of denial is to minimize your loss. Spiritual people do this effortlessly because they have Bible based clichés ready to do the job. What do we say when confronted with loss? *I'm just trusting the Lord. The Lord gives, and he takes away.* You can fill in your own personal favorite.

The problem with clichés isn't that they are untrue but that they shut down the thinking and grieving process. You should absolutely trust in the Lord. He will bring you through your loss. BUT, it still hurts. It's still a loss. You can't just act like nothing happened and move on with your life. You need to acknowledge your loss, admit the impact it has on you, give yourself permission to feel terrible about it for a season, and resolve the issues that come from the loss. THEN you can move on, but not before.

This process I just described isn't sin, like some Christians think it is. Instead, this process is called "being human" which is how God made us. We hurt, we feel pain, and we get sad. It's okay. It's necessary. But church people don't always give themselves permission to be human. They think they have to be above human emotion, and so they spiritualize their loss by trivializing it. What they don't realize is their loss then sits in their heart rotting for years, souring them on life. It sends out shock waves of anger and depression every so often but since the loss is buried so deep, they never make the connection. They blame their feelings on current irritations, when in reality; the emotions are linked to previous loss.

If you are in ministry, I hope you realize that losses automatically come with your calling. I'll talk about this in coming days. But for now, start to ask yourself what your losses are, and then what emotions you have in response to the losses. Once you can answer those questions, it would be great for you to share your losses with God first, and then your spouse, friend, or counselor, which will help you to start moving out of exile.

What about you?

- *What are some ways you have denied your losses?*

- *What are some clichés you use to minimize loss?*

- *What keeps you from giving yourself permission to face your losses?*

- *Do you think it is sin to allow yourself to feel the pain of loss and grieve it?*

JOURNALING

The evidence is mounting that the act of writing about traumatic experience for as little as fifteen or twenty minutes a day for three or four days can produce measurable changes in physical and mental health. James Pennebaker

In Day Ten, I talked about denial and how we often minimize our losses by over spiritualizing them. But a woman told me that she often had the opposite problem. She had too much emotion. Rather than minimize and deny her losses, she would obsess over them, allowing them to consume her life. She needed to find ways to channel her emotion in positive ways. She said journaling was one positive approach she took.

I recently came across some interesting research in Brene Brown's book, *Daring Greatly*, which relates to journaling:

> *In a pioneering study, psychologist and University of Texas professor James Pennebaker and his colleagues studied what happened when trauma survivors— specifically rape and incest survivors— kept their experiences secret. The research team found that the act of not discussing a traumatic*

event or confiding it to another person could be more damaging than the actual event.

Conversely, when people shared their stories and experiences, their physical health improved, their doctor's visits decreased, and they showed significant decreases in their stress hormones. Since his early work on the effects of secret keeping, Pennebaker has focused much of his research on the healing power of expressive writing.

In his book, Writing to Heal, *Pennebaker writes, "Since the mid-1980s an increasing number of studies have focused on the value of expressive writing as a way to bring about healing. The evidence is mounting that the act of writing about traumatic experience for as little as fifteen or twenty minutes a day for three or four days can produce measurable changes in physical and mental health. Emotional writing can also affect people's sleep habits, work efficiency, and how they connect with others."* (p. 82) Penguin Group

Brown notes the Alcoholics Anonymous saying: *you are only as sick as your secrets;* her point being that it's important to process your pain with someone, even if it's yourself through journaling. Everyone needs an outlet to vent their thoughts and emotions without apologizing for them. Once you get your thoughts down on paper, you can start to admit how you really feel and deal with your losses effectively.

Some people don't want to talk or journal about their problems for fear they aren't trusting God. They think they shouldn't need these outlets. All they need is God. Well, *hello.* Maybe God wants to give them some tangible outlets to help process their problems. It's not a sign of weak faith to want, or need, to share your pain and resolve it.

What about you?

- *Are you a journaler? Why or why not? If so, how has it helped you to process loss?*

- *What other ways have you found helpful to share your pain in constructive ways?*

- Consider journaling for a week to see if it offers you any help.

DAY 12

SECONDARY LOSSES

There are two levels of loss: a primary loss and a secondary loss.

Many people get stuck in exile due to their anger that comes from a painful loss. But you should know that there are two levels of loss: a *primary* loss and a *secondary* loss.

Here's a simple example...do you ever lose your car keys? Well, I do. It drives me crazy. I get so mad at myself. One time I stopped and asked myself why that is. I mean, I know I will find them eventually (usually in my pocket). They are obviously in the house. Why the anger? What's the big deal?

It dawned on me that I get mad because of the *secondary* losses. The secondary losses are those that come as a *result* of losing my car keys. For example; I didn't just lose the keys, I lost time looking for them. Now I'm late. That leads to more loss. Because I'm late, I lose my sense of calm. When my wife tries to help me, I vent my frustration on her, losing my connection with her. When I finally find my keys, I drive faster, which might end in a speeding ticket. Now I lose money. When I walk into work late I might lose respect. People say...*Remy's late again...I can never count on him.*

This is a simple analogy, but do you see what I'm saying about secondary losses? It's not just losing your keys that is so upsetting. It's all the other losses that come with the loss of the keys: real or imagined. If I had to assign responsibility for my emotion, I'd say that only 20% of my anger has to do with the lost keys and 80% has to do with the losses *associated* with the keys. So *that's* why I get so mad. This insight was an "aha moment" for me.

Now, take that example and apply it to what I've said about the bigger losses in life: loss of a loved one, loss of a ministry, loss of your marriage, etc. (the list is endless). Each of these events, on their own, is painful but they represent only 20% of the real issue.

Many people never see the bigger issues. They see the "car keys." They don't see the "loss of respect." So they spend their time lamenting the keys, blaming the keys, blaming their wife who is no help in finding the keys, asking God to give them new keys, etc. They think they are in exile because of the keys. Hardly. The "keys" are not the issue. Helping you regain your "keys" isn't what God is after. He's after something much deeper in you.

Flipping back to real life, if you lost your ministry, that's painful. But don't over focus on the primary loss. What really hurts are the secondary losses: the loss of respect from the people who voted you out, the loss of control because you couldn't do anything to stop it, the loss of income and the esteem that comes from being able to provide for your family, the loss of your ministry dream to transform lives, or the loss of purpose now that you don't have an office to go to on Monday morning.

Whether you see this or not will determine if you ever make it out of exile. For me, this understanding became a defining moment in my life. I now quickly look past the primary loss to ask myself deeper questions like: why do I need to be respected by those who rejected me? Why do I need to be in control? Do I really think God has failed me? These are the kinds of questions that lead to deep insight and provide a way out of exile.

What about you?

- You are probably aware of the primary losses in your life. Write them down. *Now, what are the secondary losses associated with each primary loss?*

INVALIDATION

People don't understand pastors or what it means to be in ministry. We are set up to be invalidated.

In Day Twelve I talked about secondary losses and how not knowing about them can leave you in exile. Over the next few days, I want to talk about four categories of primary loss and the secondary losses that accompany them. Remember, a primary loss is like "losing your car keys" while the secondary loss is how "losing your cars keys" affects you emotionally.

Primary Loss #1: Invalidation

The first category of loss is invalidation. To invalidate someone is to insult them or put them down. It means to disrespect or discredit someone, often causing them to feel worthless.

Simon Cowell made a name for himself invalidating people on the TV show, *American Idol*. His put-downs drew boos and cat-calls from the audience. You could often see the contestants visually wilt on stage, wishing they could find a hole to crawl in.

If you are a pastor, you are an easy target for the mini-Simon Colwell's who are in your congregation. I asked pastors on a Facebook page how they felt invalidated and these are some of their responses:

- I've had several variations of this conversation: *"So you're a pastor?"* (Oh, how interesting, a female pastor, tell me more). "Yes, I work primarily with the youth at the church." *"Oh, you're a YOUTH pastor."* (Oh, just a youth pastor, as if that somehow makes my credentials not as legitimate).

- *It must be nice to work one hour a week.*

- *A pastor... Right, preach a sermon and then back to drinking coffee... All you do is drive around and socialize with people, what an easy job.*

- First compliment I ever received from a member (who actually went to the trouble to use the phone): *"Great job getting us out of there on time today pastor."*

- *"Oh, you're a chaplain? I could never be a chaplain. I could not compromise the word of God."* (Spoken by someone uncomfortable with my ministry to non-Christians in the hospital.)

- Someone asked for financial assistance we couldn't give and said, *"You pastors don't know what it's like to have to work for a living."*

- My wife and I often find ourselves excluded from social gatherings. We'll hear of groups that get together for parties, or to catch a game, or a night out for drinks...and we just never got invited (even though we would consider these people friends). I think, in their minds, having the pastor along would be weird, if not a complete killjoy.

- We served a church for three years. The church doubled in size. Everything was going great. New youth group and plans to build and hire a youth pastor. One night the elders decided they wanted the church to remain small and asked me to resign. They said we ruined their quiet country church with all the "new" people. They've been through three other pastors in the last two years since we left. It was, and has been, heartbreaking. 40 people have been displaced.

My personal sense of invalidation is when people ask me what I do for a living. That's a guaranteed conversation stopper. Last year my wife and I traveled to Glacier National Park via train. They often seat you with other passengers for supper. As we greeted people, and introduced ourselves to each other at our table, I decided to expand my typical answer (*I'm a pastor*) to give people more opportunities to follow up with a question for me. This time I said: *I'm a writer, speaker, addiction consultant, and I pastor a church.* Surely, one of these options would invite a follow-up question and interesting discussion. It didn't. I got the same blank look as usual, and the conversation quickly shifted.

People don't understand pastors, or what it means to be in ministry. We are set up to be invalidated. People rarely give us the credit we deserve. It's demeaning. If you are not prepared to be invalidated, life will be cruel to you. But invalidation is only the primary loss. What's the secondary loss associated with being invalidated? One loss is the loss of respect. Everyone wants their value recognized. No one wants their life's work to be trivialized.

A second loss is the loss of control. You want to stop people from saying stupid things. Or, in my case, I want so much for someone to show a shred of interest in the life of a pastor. Just once it would be nice for someone to lean forward and say, "Wow. That's really interesting. What's that like, getting to work with hundreds of people, talking about some of the most important issues in life?" But I have no control over what people say, or don't say to, and that's a loss.

What about you?

- *What are some ways you experience invalidation?*

- *What are the secondary losses that you struggle with?*

LIMITED CHOICES

The more choices you have, the more power and control you feel. Take that power away, and it hurts.

On Day Thirteen, I looked at the pain of being invalidated. Let's look at another loss.

Primary loss #2: Limited Choices

Whenever your choices are limited, that's a loss. You have fewer options to choose from, and everyone likes options! If I tell my five-year-old to pick out *one* candy bar from the wall of one hundred choices, he may lament the "loss" of 99 candy bars more than he celebrates the possession of one. He doesn't like his choices to be limited. It's human nature to focus on what you can't have instead of what you do have.

The more choices you have, the more power and control you feel. Take that power away, and it hurts. When someone puts you in a position where you have fewer choices it complicates your life. It's like you are in a card game and you only get dealt half a hand. Or, it's like being forced to work with one hand tied behind your back. It puts you at a huge disadvantage and the loss can make you mad.

If you are in ministry, the minute you chose the ministry, you limited your choices in life; you took on loss, whether you knew it or not. For example, a pastor friend of mine was struggling financially and he realized that, short of getting another job, he didn't have any way to increase his income. Working longer hours or working harder made no impact on his income like it does in some professions. He was stuck financially and he was mad about it.

So, becoming a pastor might mean the loss of an upside to your income. With a limited income, you are limited in all kinds of purchases: from your car, to your house, to the kind of vacations you can take, to the level of health insurance you can afford, to opportunities for your children, and much more.

Becoming a pastor means you give away your weekends...for life. I don't know about you, but I rarely do anything on Saturday, and when I do, I'm preoccupied. My mind is focused on my Sunday message, and I'm of little good until Sunday afternoon (when I typically take a nap to recover from sermon preparation and delivery, yet another loss!).

Becoming a pastor means you'll never have a normal holiday (I'm thinking of primarily Christmas and Easter). You'll always come late to the party, maybe day's late, if at all. And when you finally arrive, most people are gone and you are too tired to care.

LIMITED CHOICES

Becoming a pastor means you automatically give up some of your evenings and Saturdays because that's when people are free to meet.

Becoming a pastor means you'll never get to see the kickoff on Sunday, a luxury that people take for granted. I know it's a small thing, but I'm trying to help you understand that ministry causes losses of all shapes and sizes.

If you live in a parsonage (a house provided to pastors) you don't have *limited* choice; you have no choice! That's a loss. People might think you are ungrateful for mentioning any disappointment with the house, since it is "free" after all, but how many people would want to live in a house that was assigned to them?

Start adding up these losses and the grand total can make you feel boxed in. Welcome to exile. You'll feel anger and probably show it, but don't look for a quick answer. Finding a solution might mean more than getting a raise or more time off. Consider the secondary losses. What is behind the anger over the losses in ministry?

There are at least a few secondary losses related to the loss of limited choices. One is the loss of control. Dallas Willard talks about the importance of a person having the ability to control their lives:

> *In creating human beings God made them to rule, to reign, to have dominion in a limited sphere. Only so can they be persons. Any being that has say over nothing at all is no person... They would be reduced to completely passive observers who count for*

49

nothing, who make no difference. Dallas Willard, The Divine Conspiracy, p. 21

When your choices are limited, you can feel diminished as a person. You lose your sense of freedom and independence: your ability *to have dominion in a limited sphere.* This is why a parsonage is not always the "free gift" that you might think it is. It comes with a price tag.

What about you?

- *Can you think of other losses that follow limited choices?*

- Think through your life. *Where have your choices been limited?* Those are the primary losses. *Then think deeper; what are the emotional losses associated with those limited choices?* Those are the secondary losses. Besides control, other secondary losses might be; respect, freedom, self-image, sense of identity, creativity, progress, etc.

- Bring all of these losses to God. Tell him how you feel. Ask him to speak to you about these losses. *What does God want you to know about these primary and secondary losses?*

DAY 15

PERSONAL TRAUMA

Many people live with the unrealistic belief that they live in an impervious bubble that protects them 24/7. Other people are subject to the cruelties of life. Not them.

Primary Loss #3: Personal Trauma

In his book, *A Grace Disguised*, Jerry Sittser tells the story of how three members of his family were taken in one tragic car accident. This is what he said about loss after experiencing his own:

> *We live life as if it were a motion picture. Loss turns life into a snapshot. The movement stops; everything freezes. We find ourselves looking at picture albums to remember the motion picture of our lives that once was but can no longer be.*

Loss turns life into a snapshot. That's an interesting analogy. Lenore Terr, author of *Too Scared to Cry*, uses another film analogy:

> *The memory of trauma is shot with higher intensity light than is ordinary memory. And the film doesn't seem to disintegrate with the usual half-life of*

ordinary film. Only the best lenses are used, lenses that will pick up every last detail, every line, every wrinkle, and every fleck. There is more detail picked up during traumatic events than one would expect from the naked eye under ordinary circumstances.

That's what happened with Sittser. His life was moving along fine, like a motion picture, until the car crash. Then he was handed a high-definition snapshot of loss to always remind him of what once was, but can no longer be.

He comments on how anger relates to loss:

Anger is simply another way of deflecting the pain, holding it off, fighting back at it. But the pain of loss is unrelenting. It stalks and chases until it catches us. It is as persistent as wind on the prairies, as constant as cold in the Antarctic, as erosive as a spring flood.

What a vivid picture of the pain of loss. Maybe that has happened to you: the death of a loved one, the loss of your job, loss of your ministry, the end of a marriage, a miscarriage, physical and emotional burn-out, or any life altering setback. Remember: it's not just the loss that sends you into exile. It's the *secondary* losses associated with the setback.

So what are some of the secondary losses associated with trauma? One of the biggest losses is the sudden realization that life is not safe and predictable; you have no control. You are vulnerable to the whims of nature and the choices other people make.

Many of us live with the unrealistic belief that we live in an impervious bubble that protects us. *Other* people are subject to the cruelties of life. *Not us.* When trauma finally strikes, our bubble bursts and it sends us reeling. Not only is there a loss of a sense of safety and control when this happens, but often a loss of faith. Why would God let this happen? Can you relate?

What about you?

- *What kind of snapshots have you been holding that have kept you in emotional exile?*

- *What are the secondary losses you've experienced as a result of trauma?*

DAY 16

BITTERSWEET

One moment I am overwhelmed with thankfulness,
the next, filled with disappointment.

When I first posted my thoughts on loss and trauma on my blog series, I received an email from a friend whose son was diagnosed with brain cancer last year. The boy had a tumor removed successfully, but the following year was a trying time as the family worked their way through both radiation and chemo treatments.

I thought her expression of the pain and joy of this year captured the essence of what it means to be in exile:

Life is full of blessings and heartaches. At times, I look at my son and feel joy and praise for the progress he has made. Moments later I look at his precious bald head and am filled with the deepest sadness I have ever felt, thinking of all he has been through and still must endure.

One moment I feel my plate is full, the next I am begging God to show me my purpose in life. One moment marriage feels deep, right and intimate, the next it feels like more than I have to give. One moment my heart is full of the deepest love for my boys, the next irritation and frustration arise because the mom responsibilities feel too much.

One moment God feels so close with my faith expanding beyond what I ever could have imagined, the next moment fear overwhelms and grips me to the core. One moment I am overwhelmed with thankfulness, the next filled with disappointment.

Persevering this journey is hard. Almost a year later I am left to truly depend on God's promises that he will be strong enough and loving enough to grow me up through this journey and that all things will work for the good for those who love the Lord.

My heart is heavy ...

What about you?

- *Can you relate to the bittersweet nature of her exile?* Take a minute to share which of her words resonate with you the most. Why is that?

- *Are there other contradictory feelings that you have in your exile?*

DAY 17

UNMET NEEDS

My wife ...gets a husband that has been run over, then backed over, and then steamrolled.

Let's continue to look at the losses that cause us to get stuck in exile.

Primary Loss #4: Unmet needs

In my book, STUCK...*how to overcome anger and reclaim your life*, I discuss seven primary losses[2]. The last one I'll look at here is unmet needs. An unmet need is any area of your life where a legitimate need exists, but it goes unmet by God or those you look to for help.

When I moved off our farm and into ministry I was broke and any salary would have seemed like a fortune to me. So, I was grateful for the salary I was given by the church that hired me, but it wasn't long before I realized that I couldn't live on it.

---

[2] The other three primary losses are: exposed weaknesses, irritating behavior, and embarrassing behavior.

I told the church leadership about my dilemma and they seemed concerned, but they never did anything about it. To make ends meet, I started selling my blood plasma. The senior pastor said he felt bad for me and they needed to do something about it but they didn't, at least at that time. After many months of making requests, I was finally given a livable wage.

I cleaned out my office files the other day and I came across a letter I wrote to the elder board telling them how frustrated I was that they hadn't done anything about my salary. It hurt to look back and feel the pain of that time. Have you been in a place like that? If you are in ministry, I bet you have.

Not only do we hurt when our needs aren't met, our family is hurt too. *Our* losses cause *them* losses. Here's how one pastor put it to me:

> *Coming home with heavy burdens has... brought struggles at home. My wife knows the difficulties that come my way each day and at times she gets a husband that has been run over, then backed over, and then steamrolled. Not much left, and perhaps not that enjoyable to be with. Life at home can become trying, and my family gets what is left. Not sure how to describe all that was lost at home, but I do know a significant amount of pain and loss has taken place...*

Unmet needs go way beyond finances. It might be time off. It might be the lack of friends. It could be a spouse that you aren't connecting with very well. Or it might be a ministry that is less than stellar. You have no sense of accomplishment.

But remember, these are all *primary* losses. There are secondary losses associated with unmet needs. As is often the case, one loss here is control. You can't make people meet your needs. It's frustrating. You feel trapped with no ability to alter your situation. You wonder how long it will go on. Will it ever change? Should I communicate my needs *again*? These feelings and questions are where the sense of "exile" kicks in.

Another secondary loss is respect. When your needs are ignored you wonder why people don't care. How can they just look past your obvious need? Are you that insignificant? Is your work valued so little?

Unmet needs can also result in a loss of purpose. You begin to doubt your call. If your needs aren't being met, maybe it's because God doesn't want you in that place. You might think he is withholding his blessing to get your attention so you will move on.

What about you?

- *With which of the unmet needs mentioned can you most identify?*

- *What are the secondary losses that came with your unmet needs?*

- With all of these losses, the natural emotional response is anger, sadness and often fear. It's these emotions that create the feeling of exile. *With which of these emotions can you identify?*

DAY 18

EXILE COMPANIONS

Exile is often a place of isolation. Part of the pain of exile is a feeling of being cut off: a sense of abandonment

Exile is often a place of isolation. Part of the pain of exile is feeling cut off: a sense of abandonment. You might be literally cutoff: separated from friends or loved ones by distance. Or, you might be emotionally cut off through betrayal or rejection, even though you live in the same town or house with friends, family, and colleagues.

But thankfully, in my different times of exile, God has brought companions into my life to comfort and encourage me. Here are three companions God sent my way:

People. I can point to many people throughout my life that encouraged me to keep going at just the right time; too many to mention here. But I'll mention a couple.

When we lived on our farm, we were not only very poor but our relationships with our co-owners weren't very strong. As a result, we experienced isolation in a way that was new to us. It was doubly painful because our expectation was that our relationships would be *stronger* on the farm, not weaker. Thankfully we met a family at church who had children with ages mirroring ours. They were at the opposite end of the financial spectrum, but never let that get in between our friendship. Their willingness to include us in their lives came at the lowest time for us. When they invited us over for a meal in their spacious home, it was a reprieve from our meager life on the farm and we felt God used them to encourage us.

When that family moved, God brought another couple into our lives. In fact, they have become some of our closest friends and ministry supporters to this day. Later on, when we started Cedarbrook Church, God brought several key people to stand with us, letting us know that we weren't alone in our venture. It's so interesting to experience people in these moments because they have no idea how God is using their simple gestures to keep you going one more day.

Books. I've always been a reader. During my exiles, different authors brought grace and truth into my world to make sense of what was happening. I will share some quotes from them in the coming days.

The Bible. The Bible went flat to me for several years. That was an "exile" all its own. But during my farm years I opened it again, turning to Genesis 12, and started to read about Abraham. For whatever reason, his story came alive. I saw that Abraham's exile was much like mine. I felt like I came to know him personally and heard God speak to me through his story. Over time, other stories took on the same kind of meaning for me, whether the stories were of Moses, David,

Samson or Paul, their lives are now beacons of light to me in times of darkness.

My point here is that God doesn't leave you totally alone in exile. He's got words of encouragement for you out there some place to help you keep going. So look for them, even in unsuspecting places. Maybe the person you want for a friend isn't the person God wants to use in your life. Look harder. You might be looking right past God's chosen vessel to comfort you.

What about you?

- *What companions has God brought your way in your exile?*

- *Who else might God want to use to speak to you? Are there people you might seek out for counsel?*

LAMENTATION

*We went there to experience a little bit of heaven
but sometimes life felt more like a living hell.*

On Day Eighteen, I said God sends companions to us in exile
to comfort and encourage us. One of those comforters for
me back in my days on the farm was the word from
Jeremiah, the prophet. He wrote a letter of mourning after
the destruction of Jerusalem. He understood the depths of
loss. After he reflected on his loss he wrote:

> *It is good for a young man to work hard while he is
> young. He should sit alone and be quiet; the Lord has
> given him hard work to do.* Lamentation 3:27,28

That got my attention. I was certainly working hard. (Just a
reminder of my situation at the time: I moved from the Twin
Cities to a farm in Wisconsin with two other families back in
1990. It was a utopian dream to create a Christian
community but it didn't work out that way. We ended up
working harder than I ever imagined just to survive
financially and barely had time to spend with one another.
After seven years we dissolved the community.) Jeremiah
continues:

He should bow down to the ground; maybe there is still hope. He should let anyone slap his cheek; he should be filled with humility. Lamentations 3:29,30

I felt like life was slapping me around. Nothing I did was successful. Just about everything in my life struggled: my marriage, my faith, my finances, my parenting, etc. Things broke that I couldn't fix. I'd just stand and stare at what I broke, totally powerless to fix it. Animals died from my mistakes. I can't tell you how devastating that was.

I felt like an utter failure. It was humiliating. I didn't understand why our plans for community failed. We thought we heard from God. We went there to experience a little bit of heaven but sometimes life felt more like a living hell.

My guess is, you might know exactly what I mean. You too feel slapped around and you wonder if anything good can come from it.

Jeremiah's words might sound like a downer, but they really helped me understand what God might be doing at that time in my life. I felt like God was using my experience to break me of my pride, but if I worked through it, I'd come out on the other side a better person and better able to do God's will.

You see, before the farm, I was overconfident. I didn't know that, but I was. I thought if I just worked hard enough and smart enough, and with God's help, I could accomplish anything. I could even be profitable farming! That's how delusional I was!

The farm experience revealed my overconfidence. God showed me he wasn't going to bless everything I touched just because I was a Christian and worked hard and smart.

Instead of blessing our farm experience, God actually used it to strip me. Maybe that's happened to you too. Maybe you went into your church thinking you were going to turn it around. You were going to do what other pastors couldn't do. They didn't have the skills, faith, education, or "anointing" that you do. It would be different for you. You would have this church flying high in no time. Fifteen years later, you've got fewer people than when you started.

I was miserable during this season of my life, but in retrospect, I think God was saying:

I'm going to use you Remy, but when I use you I want you to know that it has nothing to do with you. It has everything to do with me.

Jeremiah's lament isn't a total downer. Let's keep reading:

> *But the Lord will not reject his people forever. Although he brings sorrow, he also has mercy and great love. He does not like to punish people or make them sad.* Lamentations 3:24-33

I've gone into exile and returned. Now I can say, with Jeremiah, *God doesn't reject his people forever. Although he brings sorrow, he also has mercy and love.* I hope you can believe that and find comfort in your exile. One day you will also return.

What about you?

- *Do Jeremiah's words speak to you? If so, how?*

- *How has your exile experience stripped you?*

- *What are some bad attitudes that God has revealed to you in exile that need to go?*

DAY 20

COMFORT IN EXILE

The LORD will surely comfort Zion
and will look with compassion on all her ruins... Isaiah 51:3

Once you see how many exile stories are in the Bible, the Bible becomes even more relevant. Many books in the Bible are written directly to exiles: to correct them or comfort them. The book of Isaiah is a good example of comfort spoken to exiles. God used Isaiah to tell his people that their time in exile was about over. God would soon show up to reveal his glory to people that had only known trouble:

> *"Comfort, comfort my people," says your God. "Speak tenderly to Jerusalem, and proclaim to her that her hard service has been completed, that her sin has been paid for, that she has received from the LORD's hand double for all her sins."*

> *A voice of one calling: "In the desert prepare the way for the LORD; make straight in the wilderness a highway for our God. Every valley shall be raised up, every mountain and hill made low; the rough ground shall become level, the rugged places a plain. And the glory of the LORD will be revealed,*

and all mankind together will see it. For the mouth of the LORD has spoken." Isaiah 40:1-5

In other words, take courage people; your days of exile have an expiration date. They aren't meant to last forever. It's time to start looking for God to show up and bring you "home."

Exile makes you feel like a washout for God. All you can see is *your* failure, or what or who has failed *you*. Isaiah speaks to this hopelessness by communicating the restoration that God has for them:

> *The LORD will surely comfort Zion and will look with compassion on all her ruins; he will make her deserts like Eden, her wastelands like the garden of the LORD. Joy and gladness will be found in her, thanksgiving and the sound of singing. "Listen to me, my people; hear me, my nation: The law will go out from me; my justice will become a light to the nations. My righteousness draws near speedily, my salvation is on the way, and my arm will bring justice to the nations. The islands will look to me and wait in hope for my arm."* Isaiah 51:3-5

If you are in the midst of exile, God's salvation might seem hard to believe. Maybe you looked for it for so long that you gave up. You conditioned yourself to no longer look for God. You've accepted "exile" as your lot in life. Don't be too quick to accept that role. Salvation might be nearer than you realize.

What about you?

- *Have you given up on God? Did your exile cause you to walk away, assuming God walked away first? Or do you still have hope of his return to rescue you? Why is that?*

- Read through these words of Isaiah 51 again. *What are the words he uses to describe exile? What are the words he uses to describe the restoration of God? Do any of these words feel like they might be for you?*

SCATTERED SHAME

Exile is a time of stripping, but when the stripping is done, restoration follows.

One of my favorite exile stories is hidden deep in the books of 2 Samuel and 1 Chronicles. The story is about King Saul's grandson, Jonathan's son. He's given two names. In 2 Samuel he's called, *Mephibosheth* (meaning, he who scatters my shame). In 1 Chronicles he's called, *Meribaal* (the Lord is against me). These are two very conflicting names!

You have to piece together a few scriptures to make sense of the story. Here's the thumbnail storyline: Jonathan was the son of King Saul and a good friend of David. The two men made a covenant with each other. Jonathan promised to support David, even though his dad hated him. David, in turn, promised to care for any of Jonathan's offspring should Jonathan be killed.

Jonathan did soon die in battle, along with his father, Saul. When that happened, Saul's entire family fled Jerusalem, convinced the new king would kill all of Saul's descendants (as was the custom of new kings). In the rush, Jonathan's five-year-old son was trampled and lost the use of his legs. He then lived for 20 years in the desert until David, now king, remembered his promise to Jonathan and invited him to return.

My guess is that Jonathan's son went by the name "Meribaal" during the desert and exile season of his life. I'm sure it felt like *God was against him*. He went from being the grandson of the king, with all the preferential treatment that comes with that, to exile in the desert with no legs.

But his fortune turned when David sent for him. David spoke five blessings to Meribaal, which was most likely the cause for his name change to Mephibosheth (he who scatters my shame). As you listen to these words, consider how they might be words of blessing that God offers you as well:

"Do not fear." David didn't want Mephibosheth to fear retribution against his family. He wanted him to relax.

In the same way, God wants to comfort you. He's not against you. He wants you to know that it doesn't matter what is in your past. He accepts you unconditionally. It's easy to believe that life in exile will go from bad to worse. But God wants you to know that he has you in the palm of his hand.

"I will surely show you kindness." It's one thing to not fear: to believe that bad things won't happened, but here, David assured Mephibosheth that *good* things would happen, even though the last twenty years hadn't been that way.

After you've been in exile a while, it's hard to believe that kindness is possible. You give up on having good days and start being grateful for the days that are *less* bad. But kindness is a core part of God's identity. You can expect to see that in various ways.

"I will restore all the land that belonged to your grandfather, Saul." Here David reveals a specific kindness, the first of three. Imagine the wealth of King Saul. Imagine how much land he once owned. David gave all that land to Mephibosheth, something I'm sure he thought was lost forever.

Exile is a time of stripping, but when the stripping is done, restoration follows. That's something to look forward to. I can't promise that God will give you back exactly what you lost (a ministry, a marriage, finances, etc.) but he can restore good things to your life. Life *can* be good again.

"You will always eat at my table." This is the second kindness David offered. To eat at the king's table was a great honor. Only family and dignitaries were allowed that privilege. But that was offered to Mephibosheth, a former "enemy of the state," at least he thought he was.

In the same way, God honors us by offering us intimacy with him. We are now "friends of God" in spite of our past failure.

"I grant you all of Saul's servants." David offers one more kindness. Not only was Mephibosheth given Saul's land, but the servants to work the land. Although he still had no use of his legs, he was given the ability to overcome his setback.

God wants to give you whatever you need to make a successful comeback. Exile is for a season. Don't let it become the norm.

Not long after Mephibosheth was welcomed into David's household, he married and experienced another kindness: a son named Micah (meaning, Who is like God?). I'm sure that was the question Mephibosheth kept asking himself: *Who is like God? Who but God could bring me back from exile and restore me in such a dramatic way?* I bet he never dreamed that someone would marry him in his condition. But the grace of God allowed the impossible to happen...*above and beyond all he could ever hope or ask for.*

I hope this story brings some encouragement to you as you imagine how God might also scatter your shame and restore you to a new life, out of exile.

What about you?

- *Of the five blessings mentioned, do any resonate with you?*

- *Is there anything blocking these blessings from your life?*

- *Sometimes shame causes us to sabotage our restoration. Is there anything you do, or attitude you hold, that might be blocking your restoration?*

- *What kindnesses has God shown you?*

DAY 22

EXILE WISDOM

...the beauty of having gone through an exile is when, after the stripping is over, you can truthfully say...I'm okay. I'm naked, but I'm okay.

I mentioned on Day Eighteen that God gives us companions in exile. God speaks to us words of comfort through people, certain Bible passages, and authors.[3] Today, I want to begin sharing a few readings from one of my exile "friends:" Richard Rohr.

I had never heard of Rohr until about a year ago when a friend of mine recommended his book: *Falling Upward.* Since then I've been getting daily emails with excerpts from his many writings. I wish I would have known about Rohr earlier. His words cut to the essence of life and walking with God. Here is a reprint of a post from his daily blog:

---

[3] Some people have mentioned that God has also used certain musicians as comforting companions in exile.

You Can't Make Love All Dressed Up

We fear nothingness. That's why we fear death, of course, which feels like nothingness...The nothingness we fear so much is, in fact, the treasure and freedom that we long for... We long for the space where there is nothing to prove and nothing to protect; where I am who I am, in the mind and heart of God, and that is more than enough. Spirituality teaches us how to get naked... Adapted from Radical Grace: Daily Meditations, p. 333[4]

"Getting naked" might be an odd way to put it, but isn't that what stripping is all about: getting naked? The pain of exile comes from the stripping that takes place. Not only does the stripping hurt; the fear of being naked and having nothing can be suffocating. But the beauty of having gone through an exile is when, after the stripping is over, you can truthfully say...*I'm okay. I'm naked, but I'm okay.* What we feared isn't nearly the monster we thought it would be. Rohr says it's actually the treasure and freedom we long for, but have no idea how to attain.

When I was a kid my parents fought about the lyrics to a song. It was called, "Is that all there is?" by Peggy Lee. The song listed a number of traumatic events, like your house burning down. The refrain was:

> *Is that all there is?*
>
> *If that's all there is my friends, then let's keep dancing.*

---

[4] To sign up for Rohr's daily devotional visit: www.cac.org

Let's break out the booze and have a ball, if that's all there is.

My dad thought it was a stupid song because, of course, everyone would hate their house burning down. My mom saw the freedom of not being impacted by the tragedy. That's what we are talking about here.

Rohr says it's that place where you have nothing to prove or protect. Once you've been exposed in your nakedness, that is, lost it all in exile and survived, you can stop playing that game. I don't think we realize how much energy we put into acquiring status and then protecting it. We want so much to be validated: to be told that we are doing a good job and that we matter. Wouldn't it be nice to let that all go?

I can't say that I've arrived at this place Rohr calls "nakedness" but I've had fleeting brushes with it. I know what's it's like to have nothing. I really thought I might live the rest of my life in poverty and without ministry. But God met me in my weakness. I had nothing to offer him, yet he restored me and used me beyond what I ever imagined was possible. So now, instead of working to "prove or protect," I'm just extremely grateful. If I lost it all tomorrow, I can't be sure, but I think I could "just keep dancing." At least I hope I would.

What about you?

- *Have you come to the freedom of "nakedness," or are you still in the process?*

- *Does this idea of nakedness scare you, and if so, why?*

- *What is it about your exile that makes you feel "naked?"*

- *How have you resisted God's attempts to "strip" you?*

- *What needs to happen for you to let go of the fear of being "naked?"*

DAY 23

TWO HALVES OF LIFE

One of the best-kept secrets, and yet one hidden in plain sight, is that the way up is the way down. - Richard Rohr.

Richard Rohr often speaks of the "two halves of life." The first half is spent creating a box: rules to live by, unchangeable truths to help you feel in control, and markers that show success. He says these are all a natural part of development, a phase we all go through: like training wheels on a bicycle.

The second half of life is meant to let go of these constructs. By letting go of the box, you are free to experience life in its fullness. You are no longer threatened by what's outside of the box. Your thinking becomes less black and white: less in or out (he calls this kind of polarizing, *dualism*). You are less inclined to put a value judgment on everything and choose to just experience life as it is.

Rohr says that to transition to the second half of life requires an exile; a time of stripping. It often feels unsuccessful and contrary to everything you've worked so hard to achieve in the first half of life. Here is another post from his blog:

The Two Halves of Life

The soul has many secrets. They are only revealed to those who want them, and are never completely forced upon us. One of the best-kept secrets, and yet one hidden in plain sight, is that the way up is the way down. Or, if you prefer, the way down is the way up.

In Scripture, we see that the wrestling and wounding of Jacob are necessary for Jacob to become Israel (Genesis 32:26-32), and the death and resurrection of Jesus are necessary to create Christianity. The loss and renewal pattern is so constant and ubiquitous that it should hardly be called a secret at all.

Yet it is still a secret, probably because we do not want to see it. We do not want to embark on a further journey (the second half of life) if it feels like going down, especially after having put so much sound and fury into going up (the first half of life). This is surely the first and primary reason why many people never get to the fullness of their own lives. Adapted from Falling Upward: A Spirituality for the Two Halves of Life.

Exile can produce so much fear. The fear comes from what you think life MUST BE. We are afraid we won't achieve our goals, and if we reach them, we fear losing what we've gained. We resist any downward movement, but if Rohr is right, down is the way up.

If you can see the good, even in downward movement, then you've won! You have nothing to fear and nothing can stop you. You are a winner either way! Suddenly, exile is viewed as an *opportunity* for a fuller life.

What about you?

- *What is the box from the first half of your life that has kept you contained?*

- *What are some good things about the box? What are some bad things about it?*

- *What do you fear losing in life?*

- *How could (or has) exile enable/d you to experience life more fully?*

THE ENEMY OF THE GOOD

We grow spiritually much more by doing it wrong than by doing it right. – Richard Rohr

The idea of exile isn't readily understandable and takes time to sink in. But once it sinks in, everything starts to make sense, at least from a faith perspective. I hope that after 23 days you are gaining some understanding in this experience called "exile."

The problem many Christians have with exile is that they try to understand it through a secular grid of success which doesn't work. We should have caught on to that when Jesus said, "The last will be first and the first will be last," but no one wants to believe that. We want to think Jesus was being clever. No, he was speaking Truth; we are just too blind to see it.

Exile will always be offensive until we understand life from God's perspective. Here is yet another post taken from Richard Rohr's book, *Falling Upward:*

THE ENEMY OF THE GOOD

The Demand for the Perfect is the Enemy of the Good

We grow much more spiritually by doing it wrong than by doing it right. That might just be the central message of how spiritual growth happens, yet nothing in us wants to believe it.

If there is such a thing as human perfection, it seems to emerge precisely from how we handle the imperfection that is everywhere, especially our own. What a clever place for God to hide holiness, so that only the humble and earnest will find it! A "perfect" person ends up being one who can consciously forgive and include imperfection rather than one who thinks he or she is totally above and beyond imperfection.

It becomes sort of obvious once you say it out loud. In fact, I would say that the demand for the perfect is the greatest enemy of the good. Perfection is a mathematical or divine concept; goodness is a beautiful human concept that includes us all. People whom we call "good people" are always people who have learned how to include contradictions and others, even at risk to their own proper self-image or their social standing. This is quite obvious in Jesus. Adapted from Falling Upward: A Spirituality for the Two Halves of Life, p. xxii-xxiii

Rohr is onto something here. Let me try to unpack it. Exile feels so bad because we insist on life being perfect. We expect things to go "well." If you are a pastor, you expect

81

your congregation to grow spiritually, your offerings to go up, your sermons to be liked, your building program to succeed, and that you will make an impact in your community. If it doesn't, something must be wrong. Fix it! We feel defeated if anything falls short of our goals, or what we might call, "perfection." Then we are hard on ourselves as well as others, whom we perceive as failures.

But in this kind of success matrix, what do we do with failure? Where does it fit? Or do we just do all we can to avoid it and judge it harshly when it happens to discourage it from ever happening again?

Sometimes the only way to break free from this "success" mentality is to experience "failure." It can actually be a gift to "fail" so that you wake up the next day and see that the world didn't end. Life goes on and God is still God. The forecasts were wrong and there is life after failure, unless you insist on living in regret.

Rohr gives a twist to the idea of perfection saying "*A 'perfect' person ends up being one who can consciously forgive and include imperfection rather than one who thinks he or she is totally above and beyond imperfection.*" Did you catch that? The perfect person is able to include imperfection in their world. Can you do that or does everything and everyone in your world need to hit the mark?

How do you come to this place of "perfection?" You do it through failure. Until you fail you live under the delusion that you've "got it" and others should too. Until you fail you talk about grace but don't live it or offer it to others. It's only a theory. It's your theology, not your practice. But exile strips you of this delusion and grants you the ability to receive grace so you can, in turn, offer it to other failures.

What about you?

- *How have you grown spiritually by doing it wrong?*

- *How has the perfect been the enemy of the good for you?*

- *What is it about failure that enables you to offer grace to others?*

THE DISCIPLINE OF DARKNESS

When you are in the dark, listen, and God will give you a very precious message for someone else when you get into the light.
- Oswald Chambers

I've mentioned how Richard Rohr has been a traveling companion for me. Another guide has been Oswald Chambers from his devotional, *My Utmost for His Highest.* In it he talks about exile as a darkness:

At times God puts us through the discipline of darkness to teach us to heed Him. Song birds are taught to sing in the dark, and we are put into the shadow of God's hand until we learn to hear Him...

Have you seen your exile as that...a discipline...a time of intense teaching and training? Or has it just been a time of disappointment?

When you are in the dark, you lose sight of what once held your attention. When a small candle is lit in darkness, the candle becomes the focus while everything else fades to black. That's exactly what God wants to accomplish in exile. He wants his light to become your focal point while everything else in your life is diminished.

Exile is meant to help you *detach* from everything unnecessary in your life so you will *attach* yourself fully to God. As you attach yourself to God you can let go of the things you felt were so important to your survival. It's one thing to talk about God and faith. It's another thing to live it. Exile helps you live out what you've been talking about for years. If there was a better way to effect this change, God would use it. But there's not.

In the book of Hebrews, the writer refers to the priest in Genesis that met Abraham (Melchizedek). He had his own special "discipline of darkness."

> *Without father, without mother, without genealogy, having neither beginning of days nor end of life, but made like the Son of God, he remains a priest perpetually. Now observe how great this man was to whom Abraham, the patriarch, gave a tenth of the choicest spoils.* Hebrews 7:3,4

What made this priest like Jesus? It's not in what he had but in what he lacked. Read these verses again and notice all the negatives: without, without, without, neither, nor. Melchizedek was without everything that typically gives one their identity: mother, father, genealogy. His only identity was as a priest of God. Because of it, he was called "great." Are you willing to undergo that kind of a stripping to obtain that same identity and blessing?

Oswald Chambers offers this final insight:

Are you in the dark just now in your circumstances, or in your life with God? When you are in the dark, listen, and God will give you a very precious message for someone else when you get into the light. Oswald Chambers, April 21, *My Utmost For His Highest*

What about you?

- *How does this land on you? Are Chamber's words hopeful or does it just make you shake your head and say, "Right now I'm not concerned about having a precious message for someone else. I'd just like to make it through one day happy?"* Be honest.

- *What is it that God might be teaching you in the darkness that you could share one day in the light?*

- Are you willing to be like Jesus in what you lack?

FACING YOUR NAKEDNESS

*Exile forces the question: do you need anything more than God
to be fulfilled and happy?*

Exile exposes you to the core of your being. As I've already said, it strips you, leaving you naked. Exile forces you to confront who you really are, warts and all. Let's explore this a little more.

Naked is not a very attractive condition for most of us. Clothes are good for many reasons! They hide what we lack and project a positive image regardless of what is underneath. When the clothes come off and you face your nakedness, (without the trophies, achievements, resumes, or accolades from those you respect) can you live with the person you see? Can you feel as good about *that* person as you can when all your clothes are on and you are *lookin' good?*

To be stripped of our "clothes" can be devastating because so much of our identity is tied up in them. We *need* them to survive...at least that's what we often think. But exile forces the question: do you need anything more than God to be fulfilled and happy? Is all your talk about God being your "everything" genuine, or is it just one more article of clothing that you put on to make you feel valuable and acceptable to others?

When we face our physical nakedness in the mirror, we typically note how we have too much of this and not enough of that. We are desperate to modify our body in order to be found acceptable by others. It's the same way emotionally. Without the "clothing" of performance there is so much self-blame and regret. Just listen to the accusations of your inner voice: *How could you let this happen? You are such a fool. This is what dad warned you about. This will never change. It's only going to get worse and you can't fix it. You had your chance. God is finished with you now...*and on and on it goes. We naturally find coping mechanisms to cover this up.

As hard as it is to "get naked," we won't ever know our true worth until everything is removed. It's only in the depths of our failure that God can prove his unconditional love for us. Sadly, too few of us are willing to make ourselves that vulnerable and so we are never sure of our acceptance with God (or people, for that matter).

What about you?

- *How does it feel to think of your weaknesses being fully exposed in front of people you respect? God?*

- *What do you imagine people saying to you about your weaknesses? What would God say*

DAY 27

RETURN FROM EXILE

...most people think that someone has to die in order to grieve so they never think to apply grief remedies to their loss. Naming your loss "exile" gives you permission to look at loss with fresh eyes.

We have spent twenty-six days "in exile," at least, talking about it. It's time to head home. In the remaining days I want to give you some practical ideas on how to find your way out of exile.

The first step out of exile is to simply name it. One of the reasons I called this book, "Out of Exile" is because I want to give you a name for your season of loss: *exile*. Last year I spoke some of these ideas at my home church. Someone stopped me and said, "Thank you for this series," as if I knew what she meant. I asked why she liked it and she said, "I guess it just helps to have a name for what I've been going through."

That's true, isn't it? It's like going to the doctor when you are sick and they tell you you've got the latest Asian flu. There's nothing you can do about it but somehow it helps to give it a name. It helps to know that you aren't abnormal or imagining things. What you've got is common to all people and you'll eventually get over it. This is called "normalizing."

For example, last spring I suddenly lost my energy. I didn't know what was wrong. There were a few Sunday's that I couldn't stand to speak at church so I sat through my sermons. Before I spoke I felt so depleted I just wanted to cry. I had all the blood tests done but nothing was found.

In Wisconsin, when you can't find a diagnosis, people assume it must be Lyme's disease which is a mysterious disease brought on by being bitten by deer ticks. So I started researching Lyme's. It really bothered me to not KNOW what was wrong. I remember thinking; *I don't care what I have. I just want to know what it is so I can deal with it.* (I never did find out what was wrong. After two months my strength returned.)

That's how we feel emotionally too. We want to know what's wrong, so it helps to have a name for what we experience. Technically, what I've been talking about in "exile" is grief and loss. Most people think that someone has to die to grieve so they never think to apply grief remedies to their loss. Naming your loss "exile" gives you permission to look at loss with fresh eyes. Plus, there are many biblical examples of exile to reflect on and gain insight.

Now that you have a name for your loss, you can do something about it. We'll talk about that in coming days.

What about you?

- *Have you ever been concerned about physical symptoms that didn't have a diagnosis?*

- *Does it help you to have a name for the loss you've experienced? How so?*

- *Describe the helplessness of not knowing what's wrong.*

DAY 28

GRIEVING YOUR LOSS

Depression happens when you believe the lie:
Life will never be good again.

Once you name your loss, the next thing to do is grieve it. As straightforward as this may seem, we rarely grieve our losses. We get too caught up in other aspects of our loss. We might spend time blaming others, regretting mistakes, fixing problems, or wandering around disillusioned. We overlook the obvious: we had expectations for life that weren't met. That's a loss. Losses hurt. If we want to resolve the hurt we need to give ourselves permission to feel the pain of the loss and grieve it.

Let me walk you through what grieving your loss means. The grief cycle was first created to describe what happens when you lose someone to death. But these stages are true for any loss:

Stage One: Denial – Your first reaction to loss is to minimize or ignore the loss so you don't feel the full pain of it. You hope you'll wake up some day and find it didn't happen or what happened doesn't affect you. If you are unable to ignore the loss on your own, you might look for help by immersing yourself in things like: travel, a relationship, a hobby, exercise, drugs and alcohol, religion, blaming others, escaping responsibility, etc.

Stage Two: Anger – When you come out of denial, you realize the loss still exists. It hasn't gone anywhere and that leads to anger. You thought you could outfox the loss with denial. But it waited for you. It's right there, staring you in the face. Anger is the natural response. The tricky thing here is that we don't always connect our anger to the true loss. We might focus on a current problem, thinking that's why we are angry, when, in reality, it's a distant ungrieved loss.

Stage Three: Bargaining – Bargaining is when you try to take the short-cut to overcome your loss. You might plead with God to let someone live by saying you'll be more spiritual. You might promise your spouse you'll do better if they don't divorce you. You might try a network-marketing scheme or a lottery ticket to get out of a financial jam. Bargaining is an act of desperation to keep you from experiencing the full effect of your loss.

Stage Four: Depression – Depression happens when you believe the lie: *Life will never be good again*. The power of this lie is that it's close to the truth. It makes sense. If you lost something significant to your joy, then how can life ever be good again? The truth is...life may never be the *same*...but life can be good again, *just different*. It's a faith issue because it requires believing God can do this in your life; that God is good and wants to bring fullness back to your life. If you can't believe in God or his goodness, it's easy to slip into terminal despair.

Stage Five: Acceptance – Here you fully accept the new you and believe that God is with you and for you. You believe that life *can* be good again. You are not the same person you were before the loss. But even though you are not the same, you are not less of a person. You are just different. *Life* is different. Many people refuse to come to this place. They fight it. They dig in their heels. They don't want to be different. They just want their old life back. They think denial, anger, and bargaining will help. They won't. Accepting the new you is the only way to bring true peace back to your life.

Grieving your loss is a process. It takes time. There is no quick fix. Let grief do its work in you.

What about you?

- *Where are you at in the grief cycle? Where have you gotten stuck? Why is that?*

- *Do you believe that life will ever be good again? Why or why not?*

- *What will it take to get you unstuck?*

LISTEN

To be told to "be quiet and listen" is almost offensive to people who expect a solution to every problem.

I live about a mile south of a freeway. I don't think much about it. I never hear the cars. But some days in the summer, if I sit outside, I'm quiet, and think about it, there it is. I hear it. It's the constant hum of the freeway.

I hear a lot of things in my backyard when I'm quiet. If I focus on birdcalls, I hear all kinds of birds I didn't even know were out there. That's what happens when you stop to listen: you hear things you don't normally hear.

If you want to return from exile, learn to be quiet and listen. That's hard to do because there is so much "chatter" going on in the mind. There are so many things to think about regarding your situation. You think about all of the:

- *embarrassing mistakes* you made causing you to end up in exile.

- *people* who did you wrong and the ways you hope they get their just reward.

- *worst case scenarios* and how life will never be good again.

- *Bible verses* you were "claiming" but didn't come to fruition.

- *comeback plans* that never worked out.

With all of that going on in your mind, it's hard to be quiet. Sometimes we call our obsessive thinking "prayer" because we direct a lot of our thinking at God. I'm not so sure it's prayer if it's just you venting without giving God equal time to speak back.

If you want to return from exile it's important to learn the discipline of silence. Turn off your obsessions. Stop judging yourself and others. Stop planning and scheming. Stop regretting. Just shut it all down and create space in your mind for new thoughts.

Psychologist Henry Cloud says that 90% of our thoughts every day are the same as yesterday. We just keep rehashing them. We need to cease thinking to create space for new thoughts: better thoughts.

Richard Rohr talks about silence as a form of prayer:

> *Prayer is largely just being silent: holding the tension instead of even talking it through, offering the moment instead of fixing it by words and ideas, loving reality as it is instead of understanding it fully. Prayer is commonly a willingness to say "I don't know." We must not push the river, we must just trust that we are already in the river, and God is the*

certain flow and current. From *The Freedom of Not Knowing,* Richard Rohr's Daily Meditation

Sometimes we try too hard to fix our situation. We are desperate to gain back control. But maybe that's one of the big reasons we end up in exile: God wants to show us that we are not in control. He is. Rohr continues to explain...

> *...the way of faith is not the way of efficiency. So much of life is just a matter of listening and waiting ...It is like carrying and growing a baby: women wait and trust and hopefully eat good food, and the baby is born.*

To be told to "be quiet and listen" is almost offensive to people who expect a solution to every problem. But God has some things to share that he can only share with you in silence. You don't want to miss out.

What about you?

- *How good are you at silence and listening? What thoughts keep you from it?*

- *What can you do to create that kind of space in your life?*

DAY 30

ADMIT

Why is it so hard to admit what is so plain to others?

If you are quiet and listen to God, you will most likely hear from him. Really. You might not like what you hear though. He has a way of shedding light on areas of your life that you thought were well-hidden or even non-existent. But the best response to God speaking is to simply agree with him. Admit your faults. It stings at first, but it's the fast track out of exile.

Instead of admitting, some people choose to ignore what is plain to everyone else. Isn't that true? You meet someone and, in just a matter of minutes, discern a character defect. Their flaws are no secret to anyone but them. Surprisingly, what you saw in minutes, they have defended, excused, or ignored for decades. Why is it so hard to admit what is so plain to others?

A few months back I was preparing my Sunday message. I wrote in the text: "I'm a bit of a workaholic." I was going to laugh when I said it, a little chuckle to show my guilty pleasure of nursing a habit I know is wrong, yet prized in our culture.

But God convicted me that I was making light of a problem I have always had. I'm not a "bit" of a workaholic. I AM a workaholic, in recovery just like any addict. Either it's wrong or it's not. I can't cover it with a knowing laugh and hope people look the other way. But that's what we do isn't it? Rather than change, we put all kinds of defense mechanisms in place thinking that we've got people fooled. They are not.

When God apprehended the apostle Paul, striking him with blindness, his quick response was: "What would you have me to do?" He immediately recognized that his blindness was an exile given by God to reveal to him what he was unwilling to see on his own.

In the same way, the story of Samson tells how he lived his whole life blind to his selfishness and greed until the Philistines burned his eyes out of his sockets. Ironically, only after losing his eyes did he see what had been wrong with him his entire life.

My guess is you actually know what is wrong in your life. You just haven't been willing to admit it. If you truly can't see, you might want to invite trusted people to give you feedback to help you see. Either way, if you want to find the way out of exile, start by admitting what's wrong.

What about you?

- *What keeps you from admitting your character defects?*

- *What can you do to help fully admit them and begin the healing process?*

- *What do you think God is after that you have refused to admit?* Write it down. Now tell someone.

DAY 31

FACE YOUR SHAME

Shame is a deep sense of worthlessness and inadequacy that feels irresolvable. It is one of the reasons people never return from exile.

Once you've admitted your issues, it's tempting to return to denial. This happens because admitting your flaws often lead to a sense of hopelessness. You become overwhelmed at the size of the problem and unconvinced that there is any solution.

In my book, *Healing the Hurts of Your Past*, I call this hopelessness "shame". Shame is a deep sense of worthlessness and inadequacy that feels irresolvable. It is one of the reasons people never return from exile. Shame is rooted in the lies we believe, lies like:

> *I don't deserve to return from exile, I deserve to be punished.*

> *I don't measure up. My church, my family, my company are all better off without me.*

> *I don't have what it takes to succeed in ministry, or marriage, etc.*

This is my true self. I have no hope of change.

Shame feeds off these lies and creates new ones, trapping you in an ever-increasing web of lies. Once you believe them, they become your new reality. They define your existence, causing you to sabotage any success that God might bring your way.

If you want to get out of exile, you have to confront lies. The biggest lie we are tempted to believe is that our value comes from what we do: our performance. As long as you believe that, you will remain in exile because you will never be good enough to return. You will never be the perfect wife, husband, parent, employee, pastor, golfer, artist, or whatever it is you are striving to become. If achieving perfection is the standard necessary to leave exile, you are stuck.

But the truth is: your value doesn't come from what you do. Your value comes from whose you are (God's child). So here are six truths to help reshape your self-concept:

1. **God created you.** This fact alone gives you infinite worth. Your value doesn't come from what you do but by who crafted you.

2. **God loves you**. That's because God loves what he creates. It's impossible for God to not love what he creates because everything he creates has infinite worth.

3. **God accepts you**. He welcomes you into his presence. He wants you in his presence so much that he sent Jesus to make that possible.

4. **God forgives you**. Whatever your reasons are for thinking God rejects you, God's forgiveness overcomes those reasons. God washes you of every sin you've ever committed, thought about committing, or might commit in coming days.

5. **God approves you**. Since God forgives you, that means you are as perfect in his eyes as Jesus himself. There is no sin greater than God's forgiveness. You can't out sin God's forgiveness, so that means you stand before him fully approved. The Bible calls this being declared righteous.

6. **God empowers you**. God not only put you in right standing with him, he gifts you with the presence of his Spirit to help you live a new life.

Focusing your mind on these truths will help you to stand strong, whether you are in exile or not.

What about you?

- *What are the inadequacies that you are most conscious of having?*

- *Do you hate yourself for these inadequacies?*

- *Could it be that you've been stuck in exile so long because you don't like yourself very much and you feel the need to punish yourself for it?* Think about that before you are quick to discount it.

- *How could embracing these six truths help you thrive in exile or return from it?*

DAY 32

PEACE IN THE PAIN

*Peace doesn't come by having God fix what's broken.
Peace comes by being fixed on God.*

Exile can be a pretty raw existence. Nothing is settled, and it *feels* like it never will be. Peace is a distant memory. But Jesus said he came to give us peace:

> *Peace I leave with you; my peace I give you. I do not give to you as the world gives. Do not let your hearts be troubled and do not be afraid.* John 14:27

Notice that the peace Jesus gives isn't the peace that we find in the world. Peace in the world is the moment when all is calm. No problems. No worries. The peace that Jesus offers is a peace that comes *even in the midst of trouble.*

God helps us better understand his peace when he said:

> *If only you had paid attention to my commands, your peace would have been like a river, your righteousness like the waves of the sea.* Isaiah 48:18

That is, if God's people would have aligned themselves with God their peace would be unending, like the flow of a river. Combining the two thoughts...the peace of the world is temporary and conditional. The peace of God is unconditional and, therefore, never stops. That means our peace doesn't have to depend on our circumstances. We can have peace even in exile.

The average person loses peace when they experience one of three things: change, conflict, or a loss of control. When one of these happen, they usually work their way through these four plans:

- Plan A: they take back control by whatever means necessary.

- Plan B: if they can't take control, they ask or pay someone else to do it for them.

- Plan C: if Plans A & B fail, they go into denial by ignoring, minimizing, or escaping their pain.

- Plan D: if none of these work, they ask God to fix it.

- If all plans fail, they fall into despair.

Sound familiar? In one sense, there's nothing wrong with this process. It's natural. Sometimes we need our plans to fail to see God work. But it's important to realize that God doesn't always answer Plan D prayers (*Fix it! Get me out of this jam!*) because that's the peace of the world. He wants us to experience a peace that is better than that.

Peace doesn't come by getting God to bring all our chaos under our control. Peace comes when we bring all of our chaos to God and place it under his control. In fact, Isaiah tells God:

> *You will keep in perfect peace all who trust in you,*
> *whose thoughts are fixed on you!* Isaiah 26:3

Notice the source of peace. Peace doesn't by having God fix what's broken. Peace comes by being *fixed on God*.

My point is that returning from exile should never be your goal so "I can get my life back," or "I can be happy again." Exile *is your life* for a season so you need to find a way to experience peace and joy *there,* not hold your breath and run through this season hoping to exhale on the other side. Clamoring for premature peace will only abort the process that God has brought you into exile to experience.

No matter what you might be suffering today, God has a peace to "guard your heart and mind" (as Paul promised the Philippian church – 4:7). It's yours if you want it.

What about you?

- *What is your process to take back control in your life?*

- *Can you relate to the plans I laid out above? How so?*

- *Have you been asking God to bring control to your life rather than bringing your life under his control? What can you do to turn that around?*

DAY 33

BE THE HERO

*Healthy stories challenge us to be active characters,
not passive victims or observers.* - John Trent

When you are stuck in exile there comes a time to "be the hero" of your story. A negative way to say this: *stop playing the victim.*

It doesn't take any courage to be angry about your situation. It doesn't take any skill to complain, gossip, cast blame, or feel sorry for yourself. Anyone can do that. But is that the story you want your life to tell?

Would you watch a movie for two hours about a person who suffered an injustice, then complained about it and felt sorry for himself the rest of the movie? Of course not! What makes a good story is when someone faces injustice with wisdom, courage, and grace to *overcome* it. We call these people heroes. So why not be the hero of your own story?

Being the hero requires a choice: a heroic choice. It means stepping up and saying, *I'm not going to let my past control me anymore. I'm going to take responsibility for what's happened to me and move on with my life.*

Heroic choices free you from getting stuck in exile and open your life up to new possibilities. They make your story compelling. Engaging. I like what John Trent says about the power good choices have on your life:

> *Healthy stories challenge us to be active characters, not passive victims or observers. Both the present and the future are determined by choices, and choice is the essence of character. If we see ourselves as active characters in our own stories, we can exercise our human freedom to choose a present and future for ourselves and for those we love that give life meaning.* Choosing to Live the Blessing, p.36

Trent makes the case we should be proactive in choosing our future and not let our future simply happen to us. He builds on this idea of choice when he says:

> *We can curse the past like victims of circumstance, or we can bless it like victors over our circumstances. It's up to us. It's our choice. In some of the strongest and most compelling stories, the main character makes life-and-death choices. These choices give the story energy. They make the plot intriguing. They also change the character.*
>
> *The character who doesn't make choices is weak and passive. So if we want our lives to tell strong and compelling stories in which the characters grow into people of blessing, then we – the characters – have to make choices. Choices that are sometimes difficult. Choices that are sometimes painful. Choices that are sometimes critical, where something*

important is at stake. Choosing to Live the Blessing, p.66

If you think of the movies that touch you, they most often reach a moment of decision for the protagonist. In the beginning of the story she struggles with a problem, but there is a "make or break" moment. Against all odds she decides to take a risk and do the right thing.

The risk adds tension to the story because it adds a level of doubt. *Can she do it? Will she regret her choice?* In the end her choice pays off. You breathe a sigh of relief. Her choice enables her to overcome her struggle and become the hero. That's a story you are willing to pay money to see.

Think of your life as a story half written. Half the book is full. You can't do anything about those early chapters, but the rest of your book has all blank pages. You determine how your story will end. What will you write?

Remember, the most compelling stories are turn-around stories. These are stories where a person was down for the count and made a comeback, even in the eleventh hour. So never give up on your story. Ask God to help you write a compelling comeback story.

What about you?

- *Are you making choices that will tell a good story?*

- *What are some choices you can make this week that will make you the hero of your story?*

DAY 34

REFRAMING THE LOSS

Reframing enables you to be thankful for thankless situations.

In the book, *Change or Die*, Alan Deutchman says there are three factors that contribute to change; relationships, retraining, and re-framing. Change requires the right person coaching you (relationship), the right information (retraining), and to see your problem from a fresh perspective (reframing).

All three of these components are also important if you want to return from exile. Most people think that just getting good information will help. We buy self-help books for this reason. Some people realize the importance of that catalytic counselor, friend, or pastor who made the difference in their change. What we often lack is the right perspective. The information and relationships don't help if we don't have the right perspective and actively reinforce it.

The term "reframing" comes from the idea that you can often change the meaning of a picture by adjusting the frame. Imagine a picture of people enjoying a beach but there is a storm building in the distance. You can put the frame around the storm and call it a terrible day. Or you can put the frame around the beach scene and see the joy of it. It's all in the framing.

There is an example of the apostle Paul reframing his experience in a letter he wrote to the Corinthian church in Greece. The church was encountering great persecution for its faith. Paul too had suffered greatly. He relates to them his perspective on his personal "exile:"

> God...comforts us in all our troubles, so that we can comfort those in any trouble with the comfort we ourselves have received from God...In our hearts we felt the sentence of death. But this happened that we might not rely on ourselves but on God, who raises the dead. See 2 Corinthians 1:3-10

Paul reframes his suffering as an *opportunity* to learn how to be comforted by God so he might pour out the same comfort to others that suffer. He refuses to play the victim, complain, or feel sorry for himself. He trusts there is a greater good that God has for him, even if he can't see it.

Did you notice what he added about the "God who raises the dead?" That's key to his reframing. Every person in exile needs to believe that God is a god of resurrection. That means you believe God can do anything at any moment to turn around your life.

Reframing enables you to be thankful for seemingly thankless situations. I just finished watching a documentary on Steve Jobs. The narrator mentioned how Jobs softened as he aged. When asked why that was, Jobs said: *Failure.* His failures made him a better person, and for that he was thankful. I'm sure he didn't see failure as a blessing when it first happened. That took reframing his experiences.

In a recent Time magazine article remembering Nelson Mandela, Mandela was once asked what happened to him after 25 years in jail. He said, "*I matured.*" Like Jobs, Mandela was able to see the value in a time of exile by reframing his experience.

What about you?

- *How can you reframe the exile that you are in?*

- *What is it that God is working in you (or wants to) that you can start receiving and thanking him for today?*

- *Do you believe God can resurrect you from your exile experience?*

DAY 35

REFRAMING YOUR OFFENDER

People who refuse to forgive...think they have taken back control but in reality their world has gotten smaller. They have sent themselves farther into exile, maybe to never return.

In addition to learning how to reframe your loss, it's also important to reframe anyone who has caused you to enter exile, that is, your offender.

Reframing your offender involves forgiveness. We often frame our offender as the winner in a conflict. We frame them as the one in control while we are the one who is powerless: the loser. These pictures need to change.

When we've been offended, we mistakenly think anger and resentment toward our offender is a means to balance the power deficit. They hurt us so we hold them in contempt. We refuse to forgive them unless they fulfill our demands.

But instead of giving us control, our resentment gives our offender control over us. As long as we think they owe us, we are obligated to resent them. This only prolongs our time in exile. What we need is to be free of any anger or resentment toward our offender. We obtain this freedom by forgiving.

Forgiveness doesn't excuse the offense. It simply frees you from the need to provide payback of any kind. It enables you to close the book on the past chapters of your life and give your full attention to the present moment and the future. Isn't it bad enough that your offender stole from you? Do you really want to give them more space in your brain, even for a minute?

Miraslov Volf describes forgiveness as absorbing wrong. He says:

> Hanging on the cross, Jesus provided the ultimate example of his command to replace the principle of retaliation ("an eye for an eye and a tooth for a tooth") with the principle of nonresistance ("if anyone strikes you on the right cheek, turn the other also") (Matthew 5:38-42). By suffering violence as an innocent victim, he took upon himself the aggression of the persecutors. He broke the vicious cycle of violence by absorbing it, taking it upon himself. He refused to be sucked into the automatism of revenge... Exclusion and Embrace, pages 291-292

People who refuse to forgive think in terms of scarcity. In their mind, they've lost something that can't be replaced. They are forever at a loss and their only play in response to their loss is to ward off future attacks with anger and various forms of payback. They don't realize what they've done to themselves. They might think they have taken back control but in reality their world has gotten smaller. They have sent themselves farther into exile, maybe to never return.

A faith-filled person doesn't think in terms of scarcity. They believe in a God who can fill up what is lost by any offense. He can even raise the dead. By reframing their offender, they absorb the losses of life and are free to leave their exiles.

What about you?

- *Could unforgiveness be keeping you in exile? Maybe you not only need to reframe your offender but reframe God as well. God needs to be framed as someone who can help you absorb your offenses and take back your life.*

- If forgiveness is an issue for you, there are many posts on readingremy.com addressing this. The book STUCK...*how to overcome your anger and reclaim your life* takes an in-depth look at forgiveness as well.

DAY 36

REFRAMING YOUR IDENTITY

If you insist on clinging to old identities, you will never be able to receive the new identity, life, and experiences God has for you.

What often keeps people stuck in exile is a loss of identity. The loss they experience in exile is so disillusioning they don't know who you are any more. Therefore, in addition to reframing your loss and your offender, it's also important to reframe your identity in order to return from exile.

What people often fail to see, and fail to accept, is their loss changed them. For example, if you got a divorce, you are now single, whether you like it or not. You have a new box to check off on forms: single. Or maybe you lost your job. Your identity used to be as a pastor, and now you are...well, you aren't so sure. Are you a pastor who is currently selling cars? Or are you a salesman who used to be a pastor?

Because people don't like their new identity, they often get stuck in blame, self-pity, and denial: finding ways to dismiss or minimize their new status.

There's a better way to identify yourself rather than married, single, being a pastor or a salesman, etc. You are simply God's child. You are loved by a caring Father who is committed to bring you to a better place. If you insist on clinging to old identities, you will never be able to receive the new identity, life, and experiences God has for you.

When a person is able to find their identity apart from other people, or their associations (work, hobby, etc.), we call them "differentiated." They are able to distinguish themselves from whom they know or what they do. If you want to leave exile, differentiation is imperative.

Jesus was differentiated. He found his identity in God alone. He said:

> If I give honor to myself, that honor is worth nothing. The One who gives me honor is my Father... John 8:54 NCV

Jesus tells us he didn't look to others for affirmation or identity. His worth came from God. In another place, Jesus chided the people of his day on this point saying:

> How can you believe since you accept praise from one another, but do not seek the praise that comes from the only God? John 5:44

In other words, we too often find our worth in what other people have to say about us and not in what God says about us.

Jesus' words show us he was differentiated. He didn't allow himself to be defined by his work or ministry or family status. No one could intimidate him because he only listened to what his Father said about him. His goal was never to keep people happy. As a result, he was never devastated when people rejected him. Even in his death, he was able to say,

Father forgive them for they do not know what they are doing. Luke 23:34

What about you?

- *Take a look in the mirror. What or who defines you? What frames your identity? What is the label you hang on that picture? Is it keeping you from returning from exile?*

- *How have you been hurt by the things people have said about you in exile? How have they misjudged you? How would finding your identity in God alone change that?*

No matter what has happened to you; no matter what you've lost, you are God's child. That is how you ought to frame yourself and that is the title you should place on your picture.

DAY 37

REFRAMING GOD

A scarcity mindset holds God in contempt. Whether you mean to or not, you imply that God is not enough. He is not sufficient for your need.

Several years ago I lamented the life of someone I was counseling. It didn't seem like they would ever climb out of the hole they were in. Their life was a series of tragedy and loss. Then I remembered Psalm 23 where David said of God, "...he restores my soul." It struck me that those words were either true or false. Did I believe God was a restorer of souls or not? I believed he was.

I'm convinced many people stay stuck in exile because of a low view of God. For whatever reason, they don't believe God is a restorer of souls, and they pay the price for it.

My last recommendation for reframing your exile has to do with choosing to see God as a god of abundance, not scarcity. How do you view God? Do you expect him to show up on your behalf or do you always assume the worst; that he will leave you high and dry?

- Scarcity is about fear. You fear there won't be enough: enough money, enough love, enough time, and enough forgiveness: whatever it is you need in life.

- Scarcity focuses on what little you have; it's all you'll get, and if you aren't careful you will even lose that.
- Scarcity is about walls and locks and secrets and hiding because you can never be too careful to guard your meager holdings.
- Abundance is the opposite. Abundance is about hope. Abundance sees opportunities when others are cutting back and preparing to throw in the towel.

Have you ever noticed how many seeds a tree throws off every year? Literally thousands. One tree sheds enough seeds to create a forest. God has wired abundance and prosperity into his creation. If he's done that for trees, won't he do it for his children?

In the wanderings of the Sinai Wilderness, God's people doubted his goodness. They doubted he would meet their needs. God responded:

> *How long will these people treat me with contempt? How long will they refuse to believe in me, in spite of all the signs I have performed among them?* Numbers 14:11

A scarcity mindset holds God in contempt. Whether you mean to or not, you imply that God is not enough. He is not sufficient for your need.

Paraphrasing Numbers 14, God responded by saying: *Okay. It's your choice. If you don't think I can help you overcome the obstacles, then fine, don't enter the Promised Land. And* in fact, they didn't enter. They wandered in the Sinai Peninsula for forty years. It didn't have to be that way. They had a choice.

In contrast to their contempt, Abraham trusted God. He believed in a God of abundance: the God of resurrection. Paul wrote that Abraham believed in:

> ...the God who gives life to the dead and calls things that are not as though they were. Against all hope, Abraham in hope believed and so became the father of many nations ... Without weakening in his faith, he faced the fact that his body was as good as dead—since he was about a hundred years old—and that Sarah's womb was also dead. Yet he did not waver through unbelief regarding the promise of God, but was strengthened in his faith and gave glory to God, being fully persuaded that God had power to do what he had promised. This is why "it was credited to him as righteousness." Romans 4:17-22

We serve the God who gives life to the dead and calls things that are not as though they were.

I know there are exceptions. I know all stories don't end in resurrection and deliverance in this life. But God is a god of abundance. Why not expect and hope for the best? Why not expect something amazing...even if that's an amazing sense of peace and joy in your exile?

Maybe you are in a hopeless place. But did you see what Abraham did? It says... *against all hope, Abraham believed in hope*... and as a result of his hope, he became the father of many nations.

You are not a fool to hope. You are a person of faith.

What about you?

- *Contempt is a strong word. Do you think you've held God in contempt for not delivering you from exile?*

- *What do you think it will take for you to be able to believe God can give you new life?*

DAY 38

TRAVELING COMPANIONS

Some people like exile. They like the drama...they have no intention of returning; they just hope they can string you along to stay with them and keep them company.

Our 40-day journey is nearing the end. I hope you are getting your questions answered about what exile is about and how to find your way out of exile.

Today I want to talk about a touchy subject: your fellow travelers. It's touchy because the truth is you might get stuck in exile if you are afraid to distance yourself from them.

You see, some people like exile. They like the drama. They like being contrarian. They've never fit in, so being in the desert is their comfort zone. They wouldn't know what to do if life was "normal." That's fine and good, unless they are your traveling companions. For whatever reason, you ended up in exile together.

Your mistake is assuming they want to return from exile. They don't. They like to *talk* about returning. They will make *promises* about returning, but they have no intention of returning; they just hope they can string you along to stay with them and keep them company.

Meanwhile you wait for them. You hope for them. You pray for them. You believe in them...*until you don't*...until it becomes painfully obvious they don't want to leave exile. They never did. Deep down they like people feeling sorry for them. They thrive on pity and self-pity. They pride themselves on being the outsider. When this realization hits you, you get a sinking feeling thinking about all the time you've wasted on them.

So here's the hard part: you may need to walk away from them if you ever want to return from exile. I know you don't want to do that. Exile is hard enough *with* someone, let alone on your own. Plus, they always lay a guilt trip on you when you mention leaving, compelling you to give them another chance. After all, you are a Christian. Should you really cut them loose?

But seriously, walking away might be the right thing: for you and them. Your sticking with them only enables their self-defeating behavior. And besides, you won't be alone forever. Eventually you'll find other people headed in the same direction you are...healthy people...humble people... people ready to live the new life they discovered in exile.

I think you know what I'm talking about. You know *who* I'm talking about. The question is: will you walk away and return from exile or allow them to lead you in circles through the Wilderness forever? It's your choice.

What about you?

- *Who are the people keeping you trapped in exile?*

- *What steps should you take to separate yourself from them?*

DAY 39

DOUBLE BLESSINGS

Exile stripped you but God wants to make your life good again. More than that, he wants to celebrate you...YOU...in all of your weakness and failure.

I mentioned the other day that King David was confident that God restores our soul (Psalm 23). It's interesting to look at how God has restored people through the years.

A common theme relating to restoration in the Bible is that God restores you to a place *better* than before your exile, often with a double blessing. This means God does one better than restoration. He restores us and then takes us to the next level. Here are a few examples.

- Naaman's leprous hand "was restored like the flesh of a little child..." (1 Kings 5:1-14).

- God restored Job's fortunes "two-fold" (Job 42:10).

- God restored Nebuchadnezzar with "surpassing greatness..." (Daniel 4:36,37).

- God spoke through Zechariah that he would restore double to his people (Zechariah 9:11,12).

Is it too much to hope that God might restore double to you as well?

Restoring double communicates the exile is at last over, you are fully accepted, and the gate of blessing is now wide open to you. Isaiah's famous words give a vivid picture of God's restorative work:

> 1 *The Spirit of the Lord GOD is upon me,*
> *because the LORD has anointed me*
> *to bring good news to the afflicted; He has sent me*
> *to bind up the brokenhearted,*
> *to proclaim liberty to captives and freedom*
> *to prisoners (exiles);*
>
> 2 *To proclaim the favorable year of the LORD and*
> *the day of vengeance of our God; to*
> *comfort all who mourn,*
>
> 3 *To grant those who mourn in Zion, giving them*
> *a garland instead of ashes, the*
> *oil of gladness instead of mourning,*
> *the mantle of praise instead of a spirit of fainting.*
> *So they will be called oaks of righteousness,*
> *the planting of the LORD, that He may be glorified.*
>
> 4 *Then they will rebuild the ancient ruins, they*
> *will raise up the former devastations; and they*
> *will repair the ruined cities, The*
> *desolations of many generations.*
>
> 5 *Strangers will stand and pasture your flocks,*
> *and foreigners will be your farmers and*
> *your vinedressers.*

6 But you will be called the priests of the LORD; you will be spoken of as ministers of our God. You will eat the wealth of nations, and in their riches you will boast.

*7Instead of your shame you will have a **double portion**, And instead of humiliation they will shout for joy over their portion. Therefore they will possess a **double portion** in their land, everlasting joy will be theirs.* Isaiah 61:1-7

Notice the progression here. In the first three verses Isaiah tells of how God will restore the exiles. Then in verse four it's the former exiles who bring restoration to the land. And finally, the newly restored land becomes home to other exiles (strangers and foreigners). God heals us to bring healing. It's a beautiful picture of how God's love flows from him and spreads to all.

My final story of double blessing comes from the Prodigal Son. The shock of that story is that the Prodigal wasn't met with disappointment but celebration. Just as the father received back his son, God welcomes you back from exile. But more than that, he puts a robe around your shoulders, a ring on your finger, sandals on your feet, and then throws you a party. That's more than restoration. That's above and beyond what existed before. Why? To not only restore you but *celebrate* you...YOU...in all of your weakness and failure.

But, as with the Prodigal, you have to be willing to *receive* the blessing. He could have refused it, saying he wasn't worthy. But he stepped into the blessing and took on a new identity in order to live a new life.

What about you?

- *Do you have hope of being restored? Can you imagine God not only restoring you but giving you a double blessing?*

- *Is God trying to bless you now but you are unwilling to receive it?*

DAY 40

GOODNESS AND MERCY

I'm confident God not only provides a way to return from exile but longs to restore and prosper us.

Today marks the end of our 40-day journey in, through, and hopefully out of exile. Thanks for walking with me over these days as I've sought to help you process the losses, betrayals, setbacks, burn-out, and possible outright rebellion that landed you in exile.

I know the shock of waking up far from anything that looks remotely familiar, wondering if you will ever find your way back home. Let me re-quote Richard Rohr as I close out our time together:

> The soul has many secrets. They are only revealed to those who want them, and are never completely forced upon us. One of the best-kept secrets, and yet one hidden in plain sight, is that the way up is the way down. Or, if you prefer, the way down is the way up.
>
> In Scripture, we see that the wrestling and wounding of Jacob are necessary for Jacob to become Israel

(Genesis 32:26-32), and the death and resurrection of Jesus are necessary to create Christianity. The loss and renewal pattern is so constant and ubiquitous that it should hardly be called a secret at all.

I hope you see by now that loss, or what I've been calling "exile," is not an aberration. It's not random. And it's not something God only uses to punish his people. Loss comes to us all. It's a part of life we should flow with, learn from, and return from to continue on with God's calling on our lives...only as better people.

When I lived on our farm, one of the many things I learned about farm life is that death is as much a part of the farm as was life. You think of a farm as a place with many living animals. But when you are there 24/7, you soon realize death happens all around you. There is a rhythm of life and death. I'd imagine people who work in hospitals experience the same thing.

We live in a sanitized world where we quickly remove pain, suffering, death, or anything that makes us feel uncomfortable. We have lost our ability to suffer, learn patience, grieve, and then recover well. As a result we become shallow, self-absorbed people who get stuck in exile, having no idea how to return.

But I'm confident God not only provides a way to return from exile, but longs to restore and prosper us. David was convinced "goodness and mercy" would "follow him all the days of his life," even though he walked through the valley of the shadow of death. Psalm 23

OUT OF EXILE

When my wife and I moved off of our farm, into town, and back into ministry, I was surprised at how quickly the blessings of God came back into our lives. That was in 1997, and they continue today. One day I was reading through Psalm 31 where it says:

> *How great is your goodness that you have stored up for those who fear you that you have given to those who trust you. You do this for all to see.* Psalm 31:19

I felt like God was speaking to me directly, saying:

Remy, you think you wasted seven years of your life. You think the world passed you by and life will never be what you hoped it would be. But all the time you were enduring hardship, I was storing up the goodness you were missing. And now I'm bringing that goodness out of storage for you to enjoy.

The ministry I enjoy now is far beyond what I ever imagined. Through the ministry of Cedarbrook Church, Arbor Place Treatment Center, my books, and mentoring pastors, I have impacted thousands of people. I don't say that with pride but humility. I'm humbled at what God has done with someone who thought he was a ministry washout. If you would have told me this would be my life 20 years ago when I was milking cows, I would have told you to quit smoking that stuff! How was that possible?

The reality of my time in exile was that it didn't detract from my ministry; it enhanced it because *exile enhanced me.* I came out a different person and a better person. I find it hard to believe God would want any more for me than what he wants for you or any of his children. I have to believe he has goodness stored up for you as well.

My hope in writing for these 40 days, and my prayer for you now, is that you will experience the fullness of God's goodness to such an extent it will overflow from you and into the lives of others. After all, isn't that what God is working into all of us; a generous heart to reveal his goodness to others?

Thanks again for traveling with me. God bless you in your journey. I'd like to leave you with the lyrics to Jayson Gray's song, "Nothing is Wasted":

The hurt that broke your heart and left you trembling in the dark, feeling lost and alone, will tell you hope's a lie.

But what if every tear you cry will seed the ground where joy will grow?

And nothing is wasted. Nothing is wasted. In the hands of our Redeemer. Nothing is wasted.

It's from the deepest wounds that beauty finds a place to bloom and you will see before the end that every broken piece is gathered in the heart of Jesus. And what's lost will be found again.

And nothing is wasted. Nothing is wasted. In the hands of our Redeemer. Nothing is wasted.

From the ruins. From the ashes. Beauty will rise.

> *From the wreckage. From the darkness. Glory will shine.*

What about you?

- *Do you ever feel like you have wasted years of your life in exile?*

- *What are the biggest take-aways you've gotten from this journey?*

- *What are your next steps?*

- *Who do you know that might benefit from receiving this 40-day journey?*

EPILOGUE:
THE DESERT PREPARES YOU FOR A COMEBACK

No matter what your situation is today,
no matter how remote, how harsh, how isolated...
God can use it to make you grow and become strong.

We've taken 40 days to talk about "exile". Once I came upon the theme of "exile" in the Bible, I started to see it everywhere. For example, I just started a study of Luke's account of Jesus. The last verse in chapter one seems like a "throwaway" verse, a simple statement that wraps up a long chapter. But on second look, I saw another truth about exile. Luke is talking about John the Baptist:

> *...the child **grew and became strong** in spirit and **he lived in the desert** until he appeared publicly to Israel.* Luke 1:80 (emphasis mine)

Where did John grow and become strong? In church? In seminary? At the university? At a spiritual retreat center? No. In the desert...the last place we think good things can happen. Our view of the desert is a place where your strength is drained but not in God's economy. That's where God makes his greatest investment in you.

God can make you grow and become strong any place he wants to do it. No matter what your situation is today, no matter how harsh it is, or how isolated you feel, God can use your exile to make you grow and become strong. It can be the place he prepares you to take your life to the next level.

Once God has prepared you in exile, then it is time to return. God spoke these familiar words to his exiles before they returned from their time in Babylon:

> *This is what the LORD says: "When seventy years are completed for Babylon, I will come to you and fulfill my gracious promise to bring you back to this place. For I know the plans I have for you," declares the LORD, "plans to prosper you and not to harm you, plans to give you hope and a future. Then you will call upon me and come and pray to me, and I will listen to you. You will seek me and find me when you seek me with all your heart. I will be found by you," declares the LORD, "and will bring you back from captivity. I will gather you from all the nations and places where I have banished you," declares the LORD, "and will bring you back to the place from which I carried you into exile." Jeremiah 29:10-14*

Father, help my readers to see their desert as a place where they can grow and become strong. Help them to not limit what you want to do in their lives by their circumstances.

Thank you for the good things you have in store for them.
Help them to believe you are the God of resurrection.

Final Word:

I'm happy to correspond with you through email to answer your questions or receive your thoughts and feedback. I love hearing people's stories and adding to my understanding of exile and restoration.

Please email me at remydiederich@yahoo.com.

I occasionally hold informal retreats for small groups of pastors to process their losses together. If you are interested in this, or in me coming to speak at your retreat or conference, email me and we'll see what we can work out.

F. Remy Diederich

June, 2014

ACKNOWLEDGMENTS:

Since this book is for pastors I'd like to mention the many that have impacted my life throughout the years:

Rev. Peterson at Soul's Harbor in Minneapolis, Minnesota is where it all began for me. Then on to Jesus People Church with Roger Vann (deceased), Dennis Worre, and Bob Whitesel where I learned that God was a life changer. From there I worked with Doug Oyen (deceased) and Art Carter, at Eternal Life Church, as I cut my teeth on pastoring.

In the early days of faith my thinking was greatly shaped by Art Katz (deceased), a profound Jewish believer, and a friend of his, Charles Schmidt, currently at Immanuel's Church in Maryland. The writings of Gene Edwards were also instrumental in understanding what church is all about.

In Menomonie, Wisconsin I worked with John Mikkelson and Mike Peterson at Our Savior's Lutheran Church. You guys were a lifeline through a dark time. Jack Stimmel and Steve Clason were my partners at Menomonie Alliance Church. Steve, our time together wasn't long enough. I've missed you ever since you left.

ACKNOWLEDGMENTS

Kendal Anderson and Dan Maxton, at Valleybrook Church, were the spark that lit the fuse for Cedarbrook Church. Guys, your kingdom mindset opened my eyes to a whole new world and got the church planting wheels turning. Tom Nebel and Paul Johnson (CONVERGE Church Planting) both played key roles in releasing me into becoming a church planter. Paul, you gave me a huge boost of confidence. And another CONVERGE brother, Dr. Dwight Perry...thanks for your friendship.

A special shout out to my fellow pastors at Cedarbrook Church: Kyle Gunderson, Sten Carlson, and soon... Erik Gravrock. Seeing you guys develop and impact people for the kingdom is my true joy.

In past years I had the pleasure of working with Andre Oldberg, Andy Britz, and Christine Ruth. Christine is a true powerhouse for God and now serving at St. Andrew's in Eden Prairie, Minnesota. Her brother, Peter Haas of Substance fame, has been an inspiration with his passion and insight. And now my daughter is benefitting from his ministry. Love that.

More recently I've been able to encourage many church planters: kudos to Mike Shay, Touger Thao, Paul Robinson Sr., Rob Jacobson, Micah Witham, and Jamie Staples. Jamie, let's rock Eau Claire, Wisconsin with Good News!

Thanks to Bob Merritt, from Eaglebrook Church, for your mentoring and example of what it means to be dedicated to the teaching of the Word, along with Dale Peterson and Byron Emmert (Eaglebrook), Mike Brown and Jon Kramka

139

(Covenant) for your heart for pastors. Thanks to Dave Johnson from Church of the Open Door for your friendship and the wisdom you've shared with me over the past few years.

I'm fortunate to be associated with a great group of pastors through the Evangelical Covenant Church and specifically the Northwest Conference that is led by Mark Stromberg.

From afar, Bill Hybels, Erwin McManus, and Andy Stanley have guided me to see what the church can be if done well: *the hope of the world.*

Finally, I want to acknowledge any man or woman who hears the call of God and "...goes forth, not knowing where they are going," only knowing that God has called them to follow and serve. What an adventure we have signed on for! You and all the faith heroes are "...for whom the world is not worthy." (Hebrews 11:38)

May we all finish strong.

OTHER GREAT TITLES FROM F. REMY DIEDERICH

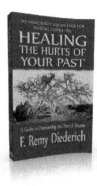

HEALING THE HURTS OF YOUR PAST

ISBN: 978-0-615-535463

Shame plays a vital role in our lives and is often overlooked. Shame can come from many things such as addiction and the hurts of our past. How we deal with those issues can be the difference between healing and rising from the ashes as a more confident and powerful person to being stuck in the same old rut.

What do you want to do? Are you reading to start dealing with the pain and find real healing?

This book is not a "feel-good" story but a "roll-up your sleeves" down and dirty look at the pain of shame. F. Remy Diederich helps you connect the dots to your self-defeating behavior and then gives you practical how-to advice about how a true understanding of God's love can free you to live the life you've always wanted.

If you have been searching for a way to find Christian counseling or addiction treatment or just repairing the damage that has been done by living with the lies and hurts of your past, Healing the Hurts of Your Past is a powerful first step to freedom.

Stuck: How to Overcome Your Anger and Reclaim Your Life

ISBN: 978-1-480-225459

We've all been stuck:
stuck in traffic, stuck in the mud, stuck in the middle...

But getting stuck in anger is one of the worst places to be stuck. It leaves you hurt and confused: not knowing what to do next. If that's where you find yourself today, then STUCK may be the book to help you get unstuck.

F. Remy Diederich goes beyond anger management and provides his readers with practical, spiritual insight into how to overcome anger. He offers helpful analysis of the question, What is anger? and then carefully suggests approaches, often step-by-step, to help you navigate the process of letting go of your anger and getting your life back on track.

F. Remy Diederich's writing is rich in biblical thought and counsel but not simplistic in its application or blind to the realities of human weakness. Issues of anger management, grief, boundaries, and how to forgive are carefully looked at from a spiritual perspective. He also includes a special section on how to forgive yourself.